REPLACE YOUR INCOME

A Lawyer's Guide to Finding, Funding, and Managing Real Estate Investments

BRIAN T. BOYD, ESQ.

REPLACE YOUR INCOME:
A Lawyer's Guide to Finding, Funding, anad Managing Real Estate Investments
by Brian T. Boyd
BUS054010 - BUSINESS & ECONOMICS / Real Estate / Buying & Selling Homes
BUS050020 - BUSINESS & ECONOMICS / Personal Finance / Investing
BUS054000 - BUSINESS & ECONOMICS / Real Estate / General
ISBN: 979-8-88636-008-0 (paperback)
ISBN: 979-8-88636-009-7 (ebook)

Cover design by LEWIS AGRELL

Printed in the United States of America

Authority Publishing
11230 Gold Express Dr. #310-413
Gold River, CA 95670
800-877-1097
www.AuthorityPublishing.com

TABLE OF CONTENTS

DEDICATION

To my wife, Dawn, who without her unwavering support we would not have been able to achieve the successes we have been gifted with. Who would have known that charity work helping Nashville Flood victims in 2010 would lead to an amazing life, family, and successful real estate endeavors?! Always the cautious one, thanks for reading *Rich Dad, Poor Dad* and telling me I was right all along about the power of real estate. I know it was difficult to say.

You're my ride or die.

INTRODUCTION

Real estate is crazy.

That doesn't mean you can't make money in it—you definitely can. You can also lose a lot, or at least waste it on expenses that don't generate more revenue for you. That's what I want to help you avoid.

Now, we all have our own reasons for wanting to get into real estate investing. Mine was that I wanted to find a way to earn money while I sleep. That is, I didn't want my income to be so closely tied to how many hours I worked, and early on, I was working a lot.

I'm a successful real estate and business attorney in Tennessee, but, as with everyone, there is only one of me. That became particularly problematic in 2015. Business was great, maybe too great, to be honest. Clients were hiring me left and right, but I was working around the clock because I had little to no staff at the time. That year, I worked forty-eight of the fifty-two Saturdays. I knew I couldn't maintain that pace—it wasn't healthy.

There were two potential ways I could deal with this mountain of work, as I saw it: 1) I could hire more help or 2) I could bring my clients with me to a larger law firm, with administrative support. Both were tempting options, but I decided to stay independent and add to my staff.

I determined that a paralegal would be most helpful, and I proceeded to hire one. She was tremendous—life-changing, really. She freed up a lot of the time I had been spending on administrative—meaning unbillable—tasks, so I could limit my work to the practice of law. Suddenly, I didn't have to work weekends any more. Life was good.

Financially, I was making money, paying my paralegal's salary, paying my bills, and putting money in my SEP (Simplified Employee Pension Plan) regularly. I had around $100,000 in that SEP at that point, but it wasn't increasing in value fast enough for me. I wanted to see growth and appreciation, but I wasn't. So, I hired an attorney, in addition to my paralegal, to help me increase capacity at the law firm, which helped increase revenue and reduce my own workload simultaneously.

Then, one day, I was hanging out with a good friend of mine, JD, and he was telling me about his business, which is coin-operated laundries and laundromats. JD is a coin-op guru, truly. As he was telling me about it, I started to see the advantages of passive income, of having your money working for you, generating even more income, alongside your day job. JD told me that, other than going in once a week to clean out the coins and perform minor maintenance, it really was quite passive.

A year later, I liquidated my SEP and went all-in on a coin-op laundry in Colombia, Tenn., which is just south of me. It was a 24-hour laundromat that lived up to JD's promise of being fairly passive. But over time, I grew tired of the middle-of-the-night calls about quarters being jammed. I asked JD if he knew anyone who might want to buy the laundry from me. He did, and I successfully sold it in 2017 for what I paid plus a fifteen percent profit.

With that money, I invested in my first rental property. I had seen first-hand the value of passive income, I just didn't want any more 2:00 A.M. calls.

When my wife Dawn and I started looking for properties to purchase, we were very open to considering units in other states—Vermont, for example. We love Vermont, I'm licensed there, but after having four contracts fall through there, we decided to stay closer to home and began looking in the resort town of Gatlinburg. It was in Gatlinburg that we came across a short-term rental property that a property manager was struggling with, so we took it over.

That property broke even the first year, which was better than the former owner did, and we bought two more, long-term rentals, in the area (3-bedroom, 2-bath units). We were self-managing our three properties, which wasn't hard to do since we live nearby, but even with that, the income being generated was closer to passive than my day job.

Those long-term rentals, not surprisingly, were more passive than our first short-term rental, so we sold the short-term unit in 2018 for a $70,000 profit, took those funds, and bought a total of thirteen homes in Chattanooga. Then we continued our buying spree, picking up a duplex in Knoxville, followed by a quadplex, and then a duplex in Chattanooga. The next few years, we sold off properties where it made sense to, and then reinvested those funds in other properties.

A couple of years into this new real estate business, I made the conscious choice to pursue active investor status, so that we could maximize our deductions. I'll tell you more about that in the coming chapters, but becoming an active investor meant qualifying to classify myself as a real estate professional through the time I spent working on our real estate business.

Today, Dawn and I are still working toward generating more passive income, but our new goal is to be able to replace the income from our day jobs. That is slightly different from pursuing 100% passive income—the emphasis is on income-generation. We're being more aggressive about our acquisitions, hiring property managers sooner so that we can reduce the time we spend managing the units, and selling properties at a profit when opportunities arise. We currently own 18 properties with 25 doors.

The good news is that you don't have to do exactly what I did in order to be successful in real estate investing. You can follow your own path and do very well, maybe even better than I've done. I hope that sharing my journey and what I've learned so far will help you replace your income, too.

CHAPTER 1

—⁓—

WHAT KIND OF REAL ESTATE CAN YOU/ SHOULD YOU INVEST IN?

You may be deciding to explore real estate investing for a number of reasons. Maybe you want asset diversification within your investment portfolio, you may want the tax benefits, you may want passive income through renting, or you may want to tap into the leverage that is possible once you own real estate. All of these are legitimate and smart reasons to explore investing in residential real estate.

These are just some of the reasons that investing in real estate is so hot right now, but that's nothing new. In fact, real estate is America's long-term investment of choice, reports Bankrate.[1] Many Americans see real estate superior to stocks, bonds, savings accounts, and gold, Gallup found.[2] Gallup[3] also found that since 2016, more than a third of Americans have named real estate as the top investment.

Zillow[4] says that the US housing market has doubled in value since the Great Recession and is now worth $43 trillion, in part thanks to a $6.9 trillion boost during 2021. Many households opted to move during the pandemic, driving up demand in suburbs and rural areas, especially since many employees had the option to work from anywhere.

In addition to families looking for new residences, demand has also been rising for short-term rentals. The long-term rental market is also booming, with the *New York Times*[5] reporting in 2021 that "single-family homes constructed expressly for the purpose of renting increased 30% from 2019 to 2020."

The biggest news, however, has been in the short-term market, thanks in large part to the rise of Airbnb, which reports that the all-time earnings of Airbnb hosts is more than $110 billion.[6] On an annual basis, the average earnings per Airbnb host is $9,600, as of April 2021. The short-term rental industry had a banner year in 2021, with hosts earning 37.5% more than in 2020, and 25.8% more than in 2019, according to AirDNA.[7]

Now is a good time to get into real estate, for the short-term or long-term. Yes, interest rates are likely to rise, along with inflation, but those factors will have little impact on you if you buy wisely.

However, if you do not currently own or are in the process of buying your first personal property, I wouldn't suggest you get into real estate investing just yet. Create some personal wealth before you try to generate additional income.

It's smart to get experience in home ownership by first living in your own place, before buying additional properties. First-hand experience is a great teacher and can help make you aware of all the maintenance and expenses that are typical for a home, and that you might have been shielded from as a renter. It's also harder to assess potential future problems or expenses when touring properties if you've never been a homeowner yourself. For example, when a home inspector tells you that you're going to need a new HVAC unit, or that the gutters should be replaced, you might not know how big an issue those are, or how much it will cost to fix them.

But once you've owned your own place for some time and are confident you have the time and energy to own other properties, jump in!

Deciding to Become a Real Estate Investor

Since the first step in real estate investing is deciding that you want to, if you're at that point, you've made progress toward your goal. Congratulations!

I'm sure your next question is, "So what do I do next?"

Of course, as an attorney, my response is going to be, "It depends." However, I will help you make the best decision for yourself. My intent isn't to give you a specific, one-size-fits-all path to follow, but to help you decide which direction to go in that makes the most sense *for you*.

One of my clients, let's call him Dr. K, decided to get into real estate investing with his wife to replace his current income so he doesn't have to work as many hours, to create generational wealth, and to take advantage of the tax benefits associated with real estate.

Dr. K bought two small houses to hold as long-term rentals and is living in one right now while his new house is being built. By buying rental properties, Dr. K can take advantage of the real estate tax benefits to lessen his tax bill each year. Investing in rental real estate has enabled Dr. K to increase his cash flow, reduce his taxable income, and create an asset that pays him every month while it grows in value.

Starting on this path to real estate ownership and investing has opened possibilities not previously available to Dr. K. He and his wife are preparing to leverage their equity in those two properties to buy their first short-term cabin rental, to create greater cash flow. The short-term rentals will generate more profit in a shorter amount of time for Dr. K. Within two years, he and his wife will have grown their portfolio to three rental properties. The couple is on their way to replacing the wife's income within five years at the current rate they are growing!

However, you should have a few things in place before you jump into investing of any kind.

One is a good credit score. At a minimum, you should be at 650 or higher. The more you can explain any drops in your score, such as for student loans, the better, too. Even better would be a 700. Moreover, if there is something on your credit that is incorrect, clear that up by contacting the three credit bureaus to report any inaccuracies.

Another is a good debt-to-income (DTI) ratio. If you're early-career, that may be harder to achieve, given a starting salary and student loans, for example. Your monthly expenses may account for 60% or 70% of your income, which is too high to qualify for most mortgages and leaves little in the way of disposable income to set aside.

There's a final piece you need to have: funds saved for a down payment on a property.

Once you have a good credit score, you've paid down a good bit of your debt, and you have money for a down payment, you can start making decisions about where to invest those funds.

Your first decision is whether to pursue commercial or residential real estate investing. While they are both types of real estate investing, they are very different in how you operate the properties.

Although I will be focusing specifically on residential real estate in this book, including the different kinds of rentals you can set up, how you rent them out, as well as other ways you can invest in real estate if rentals aren't your preference, I do want you to understand what commercial real estate is and how it works. That way you can make an informed decision about the type of real estate you want to own and operate.

When is the Best Time to Buy?

The best time to buy is now. Sure, prices might be higher than they've been in years, but they may never go back down. Or, there may be a crash next year. No one knows. All you can do is jump in when you're ready, based on the resources at your disposal. But don't jump in with both feet. Make a small buy. That way, you have less at risk to start. I always say, "Aim small, miss small." But then at least you're in the game and can start learning from that experience, to prepare for larger buys later. You cannot get your second property until you get your first. Real estate creates wealth, but not overnight. Learn while you go and make smart moves.

What Differentiates Commercial Real Estate from Residential?

Commercial real estate is basically anything that is not residential, meaning property that is not primarily to be lived in. For the purpose of this book, commercial real estate is anything that is held for business or commercial purposes. For example, the building and the land on which the building sits to house a fast-food restaurant would be considered commercial space, because it supports the operation of a business. Another example is self-storage units, which are a whole industry unto themselves, and are commercial buildings that exist to store stuff for individuals and companies for a price. They are businesses.

These are just a couple of examples when there are many types of commercial properties. There are retail spaces, office spaces, mixed use (office and residential), mixed use (retail and office), industrial, storage, hotels, and many more. There are also variations within these many types of commercial spaces, such as different classes for office space (A to C), different quality ratings for hotels, or storage space that is climate controlled or not, just as a few examples.

When you get into commercial real estate ownership, you'll be dealing with a different depreciation schedule, different types of expenses, and a renter who may be more skilled at contracts and negotiation than you are. There are permits and restrictions and different requirements for financing, too.

The difference between commercial and residential real estate is a lot like the difference between stocks and bonds. Both are investment tools, but when and how you buy them is very different. And each is appropriate for different investing goals.

Commercial real estate is also treated differently tax-wise for depreciation and 1031 exchanges (also known as "like-kind" exchanges), which we'll talk more about in Chapter 7. For now, the most important thing for you to understand is that commercial and residential real estate are different in a number of ways, which you'll want to become aware of before you decide to buy.

What, Exactly, is Residential Real Estate?

Residential real estate is where most new investors start when they decide to begin buying real estate as a business. Residential means just like it sounds—it involves owning a home as an investment property.

How people get into residential investing varies, however. Someone might inherit a house from a relative, outgrow their current house and decide to rent out their existing home after buying a new one to live in, or stumble across a property that was too great a deal to pass up owning.

But single-family homes aren't the only type of residencies that fall under the heading of residential. Anything that people can live in qualifies. That means that apartments, mobile homes, houses, duplexes, triplexes, quadplexes, condominiums, townhouses, fifth wheels, and more all can be owned as residential real estate.

Make Sure You Have Reserves

If there's one thing COVID taught us, it's the importance of financial reserves, or several months of expenses set aside. The COVID rent moratoriums meant that many tenants stopped paying rent. As a property owner, you will sometimes have to dip into your own funds to pay your mortgage payments, or you can be foreclosed on and lose the property altogether. So don't use 100% of your savings to buy an investment property. Hold back several months' worth of mortgage payments to protect yourself in case your tenant stops paying, or even to cover the time required to clean the property in between long-term tenants. Three to six months of reserves should be your target, so you can sleep easy even if rent income stops coming in temporarily.

Short-Term Rentals (STR)

One type of residential real estate is short-term rentals (STR). You may have heard about it thanks to companies like Vrbo and Airbnb. These companies have amassed fortunes by connecting property owners with members of the general public who are looking for a place to stay for a night or two. There are other platforms out there that do the same thing as Vrbo and Airbnb, but these are two names you're likely to recognize.

STRs generally provide better returns than most long-term rentals (LTRs) because of the higher prices property owners are able to charge per night. Renting through Vrbo and Airbnb and similar sites has become a very popular alternative to hotels, with price points ranging from very inexpensive to quite costly, depending on the location, rooms, amenities, and level of finishes provided to guests.

That's the upside to STRs.

The biggest downside is that STRs have drawn the attention and ire of some city councils and many homeowner's associations (HOAs). Conflicts arise when short-term renters behave poorly, such as when guests use properties as bachelor or bachelorette party pads, or college spring break flophouses, especially since some properties simply weren't designed for large groups.

Despite some of these problems, many STR investors find this area of the residential investment market very lucrative, and even worth the trouble.

Some examples of the types of properties and popular locations that STR owners rent out on a regular basis include:

- Cabins: Gatlinburg, TN; Blue Ridge, GA
- Apartments: New York City; Chicago
- Condos: Destin, FL; Scottsdale, AZ
- Houses: Nashville, TN; Lake Tahoe, NV

These are only examples, however, and you'll want to do your own research, such as on areas that you're familiar with.

In addition to buying existing properties to turn into STRs, you can also consider building.

My personal real estate agent and his wife, also an agent, decided to get into the short-term rental market. They purchased five properties that were tear-downs, meaning they were only good to be torn down and another property built in their place.

Wanting to maximize their profits, here is what my agent and his wife did: First, they bought the land. Then they went to the city zoning commission (they checked on the viability of this zoning permitting before buying the properties) and petitioned to have those particular lots zoned for short-term rental use. Once they received their permits, they tore the five existing buildings down.

Once the lots were cleared, they built two townhouses per lot, commonly called "tall and skinnies," in their place. These types of townhouses are built up, rather than out, to utilize height instead of depth for living. The floor plans had very little storage for clothing and other items, in order to open up the rooms for living and entertaining. Moreover, they added rooftop decks so the renters could enjoy the city views. They were exactly what the market wanted.

As a result, these properties are constantly rented and grossing over six figures a year. Additionally, once these properties were built, these agents refinanced the properties and pulled out their equity to be able to move on to the next investment opportunity.

While this may sound complex and difficult, it isn't as complex as you may think. This could be you!

Long-Term Rentals (LTR)

Although typically not quite as lucrative on a night-by-night basis, LTRs are a slower and steadier way to make money over time in real estate investing. In comparison to STRs, LTRs typically make less money on a monthly basis, mainly because STRs charge a much higher nightly rate. If a property can be rented every night, the potential revenue there is much, much higher. However, with an STR you're also more likely to have nights when the property isn't rented at all, when that's less likely with an LTR.

For example, a beach house rented through Airbnb might generate $500/night, whereas a monthly rental might net $8,000. If you can rent out the property more than sixteen nights through Airbnb, you're way ahead of an LTR.

However, there are also benefits of LTRs. Number one is that there is less wear-and-tear on the property and market fluctuations have little impact on what your tenant pays you each month. Additionally, LTRs have far fewer conflicts with city councils and HOAs. Renters are often more like residents and don't attract as much negative attention.

Two of the most common types of LTRs are:

- Single-family rentals (SFRs), which are standalone structures designed to house one family unit.
- Multifamily rentals (MFRs), such as duplexes, triplexes, quadplexes, apartment buildings, and mobile home parks, which have been designed and built to house more than one family at a time.

I have a client who started out as a repairman for restaurants and the equipment necessary to run the kitchens. This client grew up desperately poor and didn't want his family to live that way. He wanted them to have a better life, and to benefit from generational wealth he created.

His first toe dip into real estate was to buy a trailer park. Don't laugh, trailer parks can be exceptionally lucrative. He sold it a few years later and made a profit on it. But with that learning experience, he started buying small properties around his community for long-term rentals.

With a good stable of properties, this client then obtained his own general contractor's license and started building houses. He aimed small and bought small, keeping his risk of failure low, and grew his portfolio into a very profitable business. He currently has over 100 properties!

One night over a few bottles of wine with our wives, we discussed why he did not want to get into short-term rentals. His response was very simple: slow and steady wins the race. What he meant by this is that there is less wear-and-tear on long-term rentals, which means lower maintenance costs, lower property management fees (he is self-managing now), and he can bank on what these properties make each year. This allows him to plan better for his next project.

Don't Avoid Section 8 Tenants

When the topic of Section 8 tenants comes up, the typical response you'll hear from the general public is to avoid them, or that they're bad news, and I completely disagree. I suspect the people who are putting Section 8 down don't understand how it works, because if they did, I think they'd have a more positive attitude.

Section 8 is a state grant program that pays a portion of a tenant's rent, up to 100%, for people who meet certain income requirements. It's a voucher program though, not public housing. So, payments made through Section 8 are essentially guaranteed. It's unusual, at least in my experience, to have a problem getting paid with Section 8.

The way the state determines what you can receive for rent is based on research they do into your neighborhood. They set a standard amount that is paid, based on the number of bedrooms in the unit. Now, generally Section 8 rates are slightly below market, but it comes in every month like clockwork. And the tenants generally are well-behaved because if they do anything against the rules—from damaging the property, to having the cops called, to getting evicted—they are kicked out of the program. Since it is in their best interest to stay in the program, to get all or most of their rent paid for them, many are excellent tenants.

To become part of the Section 8 program, you have to have your home inspected, and there are very specific guidelines. For example, it needs to be ADA-compliant, which means it needs handrails wherever there are steps, smoke detectors have to work, windows and doors have to be perfect, and the heat and A/C have to be working. Inspectors will put you through the ringer to get your property accepted, and when it is, you're set as far as getting your rent on time each month.

Now, are you going to make market rates? No. One Section 8 tenant we had paid $600/month, where other tenants were paying $950, so that's the downside. And when we opted to raise the rent to $1,200/month, we gave her a notice to quit, meaning that she was welcome to stay at the new, higher rate, but if she didn't want to, she just needed to let us know. Section 8 was willing to up her payment to $660, but we couldn't continue to rent so far below market at that point.

With Section 8 tenants and others, retaining a property manager is one way to reduce the amount of time and attention you need to spend addressing any issues that come up. However, depending on the number and location of properties you own, you may decide to hold off paying someone else to manage your units for you.

Fix-and-Flip

Beyond rental real estate, fix-and-flip investing is when a property is purchased, generally at a discount, which provides the investor the opportunity to add value. "Add value" is one of a real estate investor's most commonly used terms. Adding value to a property increases the market value of the property and allows the investor to increase the potential profit made when the property is sold.

You see this type of investing on several shows on HGTV (*Bargain Block, Flipping 101,* and *Flip This House* are just a few examples to check out). Typically, the investor will purchase a run-down property, or one owned by a bank or a city, and over the course of the thirty- to sixty-minute show, they will deconstruct the property, renovate it, and then sell it to a new owner for a tidy profit. When done well, this type of investing can be quite lucrative.

The key to success with this type of investing is controlling your costs. That can be difficult unless you're planning to do all of the work yourself. Otherwise, you'll need to pay contractors and subcontractors to take care of any electrical, plumbing, drywall, roof repair, pest control, flooring, and more. While paying other professionals to do the needed work is often smart, unless you're a trained contractor, it does get expensive quickly. Make sure you run your numbers before you buy a property.

Fix-and-flips are fairly challenging because many of the experienced flippers have teams established that help them find low-priced properties and then renovate them super quick. Many of these flippers are contractors themselves. So keep in mind that those are your competitors before you jump in to this type of real estate investing.

Buy, Rehab, Rent, Refinance, Repeat (BRRRR)

If you pay attention to Bigger Pockets, or other real estate podcasts, you've probably heard of BRRRR. This house-hacking idea is brilliant in its simplicity, though I wouldn't necessarily recommend it for a first-time real estate investor. What BRRRR has going for it is that it can provide a path to achieve quicker financial gains.

Here's how it works, using a very simple example:

> Let's say our investor Pat buys a property for $70,000 in an area where comparable homes are selling for $130,000 and renting for $1,300 per month. Pat is pretty sure he could rent his for the same amount after some improvements.
>
> He puts $30,000 down and gets a 15-year-mortgage at 4.5%. He has closing costs of $3,500. His monthly mortgage payment is $332.
>
> He then invests $30,000 in improvements to the house, buying all new kitchen appliances, replacing the dirty carpet with luxury vinyl planking (LVP), updating the bathrooms, painting the exterior, and adding new landscaping. It looks great!

At that point, Pat has invested $100,000 in the house and he's ready to show it to potential renters for $1,300 per month.

Once he has rented the property for at least six months to show a steady rental history, Pat can then go back to the bank and refinance the property, taking some of the value he's added out of it.

The house then appraises for $130,000 and Pat takes out a mortgage for 70% of the loan-to-value (LTV) of the property. LTV is important because most banks will loan up to 70%, and sometimes 80%, but never 100%, of a property's appraisal value on a property. So, if a property appraises for $100,000, the bank will loan you $70,000 for a mortgage, to be paid back over a period of years—usually 10, 15, 20, 25, or 30 years. The mortgage term length then affects the monthly payment amount, with shorter terms, yielding higher monthly payments. In Pat's case, he gets a 15-year mortgage at 4.5%. His closing costs are $3,500 and his monthly payment is then $791.

At the refinance closing, Pat is given a check for $91,000. That amount represents the $30,000 he put down on the property originally, the $30,000 in improvements he made, and the $31,000 in equity he earned through those improvements. The $1,300 monthly rent check he receives from his tenant pays the mortgage and leaves him with an additional $509 to cover expenses like property taxes, insurance, maintenance issues, and HOA fees.

He can then use that $91,000 to invest in another undervalued property, or properties, and repeat the process as often as he likes.

This type of investing can be profitable, but it also requires more work to prepare the property to be rented. Investors who buy turnkey properties are able to immediately rent them out, without putting money into improvements.

Should you ever pay off your property's mortgage?

There are few reasons to pay off an investment property's mortgage, so the short answer is no. The reasons include the fact that if you have it rented out, you're probably not making the mortgage payments your-self—your tenants are. Also, you get a Section 163 business deduction for business interest on any mortgage you have and since most prop-erty values are increasing at around 2% to 3% a year, your equity is consistently growing while the tenant is paying down the note. Thus, your equity is growing faster than you think!

How I Got Started

When my wife Dawn and I decided to start investing in real estate, we began with the idea that we wanted a property we would enjoy using, if we wanted to. With that in mind, we bought a property in a family-friendly area we thought would do well as an STR. We wanted the property to pay for itself and generate some revenue, while also being available to us as a getaway whenever we wanted.

After buying our first rental property, we were honestly shocked by how much work it took to get it ready to rent, as well as the monthly utility and maintenance costs. It was like having two households until the rental season kicked off, and I was freaking out at the amount of money Dawn was spending to make it nicer.

We quickly discovered that we had different perspectives on the property. Dawn believed it needed to be nicer in order to attract higher-paying renters and thought it needed to mimic what our personal residence looked like. She completely redecorated, strip-ping it of its former black bear theme common to the locale and replacing everything from the lighting to bedding, furniture, plates, silverware, and even the door handles. She wanted it to convey more of a luxury image.

I, on the other hand, viewed it more as a stock and wanted to invest as little as possible while still being able to reap profits.

Turns out, we were both right. Sort of. Dawn was right in that the property needed to be nice enough for someone to want to stay there, but not so nice that if the Restoration Hardware couch got broken, we were out several thousand dollars.

Ultimately, we broke even the first year after the upgrades and sold it the next year for a $70,000 profit, without ever having spent a weekend there ourselves.

The bigger picture is that while the property does need to be appealing to renters, the renters do not own the property. They aren't going to take care of it the way you, the owner, will, so don't invest too much in pricey furnishings. Renters want a nice place to stay for a few days. If you can provide that, without overspending on furniture and appliances, you'll make more money in the long run.

Key Takeaways

- Be clear about why you are getting into real estate investing. What is your long-term goal? Are you after income or asset acquisition, for example?

- It's important to have a minimum credit score of 650, as well as a healthy debt-to-income ratio.

- Know the difference between residential and commercial real estate as investment tools.

- Short-term rentals (STRs) offer a high nightly rental rate, but there's no guarantee of a guest every night.

- Long-term rentals (LTRs) are a slower but steadier way to make money.

CHAPTER 2

HOW SHOULD YOU HOLD YOUR REAL ESTATE?

I have a client, let's call her Kim, who recently bought an investment property and had some questions for me about how to make the best use of it. My first question to her was, "How did you buy the property?" I was asking her if she owned the real estate in her own name or had used an LLC to purchase and hold the property.

"Yes," she told me, adding that she had set up a separate LLC for her properties but hadn't yet put this one in it.

"Why not?" I had to ask. Because the whole point of setting up a separate entity to hold your properties is to shield you from any liabilities associated with it.

Fortunately, moving properties you own personally into an entity like an LLC, a corporation, trust, or partnership, isn't difficult, but don't create that work for yourself. Figure out what makes the most sense in terms of ownership before you buy anything.

Qualifying for a Mortgage

Qualifying for a mortgage is an important step early in the process of finding and buying an investment property. You need to know how much a bank is willing to lend you, to guide your property search. If you've bought a house, you know that—for a traditional mortgage—you typically have to provide a number of documents, including, but not limited to:

- Three years of tax returns
- Three months of pay stubs
- Three months of bank statements
- A personal financial statement listing all of your liabilities and assets
- A profit and loss statement from your business if you're self-employed
- Your credit score (which the bank will run)

The process is slightly different if you're applying for a commercial mortgage, however. Commercial bankers are typically more concerned about the income potential of the property, rather than your own personal income. For a commercial mortgage, expect to be asked for:

- Your personal financial statement
- Three years of tax returns
- Three years of business tax returns
- Your credit score (which the bank will run)
- Property rental income history
- Property appraisal (which the bank will arrange)

Commercial mortgages are typically more expensive because the interest rate is slightly higher and the mortgage is structured with a 5-year term while the payments are calculated on a 10-year, 15-year, or 20-year amortization schedule, with the assumption that you'll either refinance, sell, or pay off the property after five years. That is in contrast to personal mortgages, which are usually 15- or 30-year terms.

Shielding Your Assets

You have several options for holding your property, and the option you choose will impact the type of financing tools available to you. So, you'll want to consider each alternative and its implications for financing before committing. For example, do you plan to use the property at all, maybe as a vacation get-away? Or is this solely an investment purchase? Deciding that in advance is important.

"How should I hold my real estate?" is the single most-asked question I hear as a lawyer. So, if you're wondering about this before you've bought your first investment property, you're ahead of the game. Asking after you've bought a property sometimes creates the need to make changes that can cost you money. Better to decide now.

The short answer is that there is no one right way to hold real estate. What's best for you may not be best for someone else, depending on their own financial and tax situation. To decide what is best for you, reflect on your ultimate goal for investing in real estate. Whether you want to tap into the tax advantages, generate cash flow, build wealth, or some other reason, determining your goals at the outset will guide you to the best way to own any properties you buy.

Besides your goals, there are also tax consequences to consider, asset protection concerns, and even municipal and city code factors that have to be taken into account.

However, there are a handful of entities that the majority of real estate investors use when buying properties. Yes, there are a few others that are available, but they are unlikely to be relevant to you if you're a beginning investor. Your best bet is to choose one of the following types of entities:

Limited Liability Company (LLC)

A limited liability company (LLC) may be the most popular tool for buying, selling, and holding real estate today. Why? Because the real estate owners—called "members" within an LLC—are not personally responsible for the company's debts or liabilities. Establishing a separate company to serve as owner of your real estate helps protect your personal assets from being targeted if you were ever to be sued, such as by tenants or suppliers.

However, whether an LLC makes sense for you may depend on the state in which you live or are operating. Some states are more conducive to LLCs than others; New York, for example, is probably not a state in which you want to choose an LLC because New York's tax structure is higher than other states.

Buying a Vacation Home

If your plan is to buy a vacation home that you may or may not rent out from time to time, you can hold it in your individual name, because its primary purpose is personal enjoyment and not an investment. However, make sure you get waivers and have indemnification clauses signed by any renters you do have, to absolve you of any responsibility if they do something stupid, like tripping and falling into the hot tub or crashing your canoe.

But in states where LLCs are popular, there are a number of advantages. Number one, LLCs are very flexible. You don't need to create a board of directors and they're typically member-managed. It's a much less formal structure than an S corporation, which we'll talk about in a minute, which is probably the second most common entity real estate investors opt to establish. Ask your attorney to find out if LLCs are advised in your state.

LLCs offer a combination of the corporate protections provided by corporations and the tax benefits of a partnership. For that reason, LLCs are considered a hybrid entity. And, although regulations pertaining to LLCs vary by state, some basic features hold true almost universally:

- **Articles of Organization/Articles of Incorporation**. All LLCs have one or the other. These documents are your state's minimum requirements for forming an LLC. Your Articles include the LLC's name, address, registered agent, number of members, fiscal year-end date, and other corporate facts. Once you have your tax ID number, you're in business.

- **Operating Agreement**. An LLC also needs an operating agreement, which outlines the rules of the LLC. It states what you can and cannot do. Operating agreements identify the procedures required for standard business processes. These include annual meetings, requests to view the books and records, distributions, profit and loss allocations, tax accounts, tax matters as they relate to partners, capital accounts, adding and removing members, as well as the winding up or closure of the business.

- **Resolutions**. Resolutions guide how decisions are made by the members (who are the individual owners of the LLC) regarding the LLC. Those decisions are recorded in a minute book, which is the business equivalent of a person's diary, explaining what issues arose, the discussion that was had about them, and the ultimate decisions made. Resolutions address everything from how a new member is added to how employees can request days off.

The cost to establish an LLC varies by state but generally ranges from $100 to around $500 for filing fees. Some states may even cost less than $100.

Why Choose Wyoming for Your LLC?

Interestingly, although most states publish the details of new LLCs, including who owns them, the state of Wyoming allows the members of an LLC to remain anonymous; no one can know who owns the LLC if they have a registered agent in that state. Some people choose to set up their LLCs in Wyoming specifically so that no one will know who the members are in their LLC. Other states have started to allow for this anonymity as well, but Wyoming was the first.

Although LLCs are the most popular way for real estate investors to hold their properties, there are several variations of LLCs from which to choose, depending on how many people you are working with and how many properties you intend to own.

Most people will set up one LLC and hold two or three properties in it. That's pretty typical. However, if you're going to invest out-of-state, consider setting up an LLC in that state and putting any properties you own in that state in that LLC. This eliminates having to register an out-of-state LLC as a foreign entity, thereby reducing fees for you.

Dawn and I created a parent LLC as an umbrella entity and then we created separate LLCs for the major geographic areas in which we have our properties. So, for example, we have an LLC for Chattanooga, Knoxville, and Memphis, as well as other areas, to keep them separate, but still under our umbrella LLC. It just makes it easier for bookkeeping and portfolio management to put properties in close proximity to each other into separate LLCs.

Single-Member Limited Liability Company (SMLLC)

If you are the sole owner of your LLC, yours is a single-member LLC. The IRS considers SMLLCs as disregarded entities for tax purposes, which means that while an LLC provides legal protections to you, the single member, the tax consequences pass through to the appropriate schedule on your 1040 tax return, Schedule C or E. You still have the liability protection AND you get the pass-through treatment for profits, losses, and tax treatment.

Multi-Member Limited Liability Company (MMLLC)

If your LLC has multiple members—meaning individuals or other companies—as owners, you need a multi-member limited liability company, or MMLLC. Like the SMLLC, the MMLLC is a "pass-through" entity for tax purposes. The MMLLC provides an IRS K-1 return each year to members to report the interest, share, or percentage of the profits and losses to be reported on their respective tax returns.

Series LLC

A series limited liability company is an LLC that was formed to offer more efficiency, by allowing one entity to hold multiple properties under the umbrella of a single LLC. Within the series LLC there are series that assign to each property tranche its own tax identification, books, and bank accounts.

A series LLC is a lot like a book. A book is composed of chapters, which can each stand alone as separate topics or stories. Similarly, each series within a series LLC can stand alone, with its own bank account, tax ID number, accounting records, and name.

This type of LLC enjoys the same legal protection as other LLCs, but instead of paying multiple annual fees to state agencies, it only has to pay one.

Janet, a client of mine for years, is a builder and developer. Every project she works on or gets involved with has a separate LLC set up for that project. This allows her to limit her liability to building houses on that project that are held within that LLC. Her business model was to build ten townhouses, sell seven, and keep three. As planned, she sold seven properties out of the LLC and kept the remaining three within the original LLC.

Once everything was sold, Janet made an election with the Secretary of State's office and turned the LLC into a series LLC for those three units. Each had its own bank account, tax ID number, and accounting records. This approach makes sense for Janet because she owns more than 100 units like this across the state, and this is her profession. She also has an in-house bookkeeper and a CFO in her organization. The reason this option makes sense is that her organization can internally track all of the 100+ properties and handle the administrative complexities that come along with using a series LLC. This approach is not something you should try early on in your investing career, however.

S Corporation

Another type of entity you can elect to form is an S corporation, also known as an S corp. This type of corporation enjoys limited liability, just like an LLC, and is a pass-through entity, which means that it is not subject to taxation but its members, which are called shareholders, report the income on their individual Form 1040. Any profits or losses the S corp earns are reported on the individual shareholder's tax returns.

There are restrictions within an S corp, however, that LLCs do not have. S corps are considered more formal, because of the additional regulations and paperwork that go along with them.

For one, there is a limit of no more than 100 shareholders within an S corp, and they cannot be partnerships, corporations, or non-resident aliens; all shareholders have to be US citizens. That can be problematic if you want to bring in foreign investors, for instance.

There must be a board of directors and you must issue shares of stock to the owner(s).

The S corp's profits and losses pass through to the individual shareholders on a K-1 form, as with an LLC. The S corp files a Form

1120S return with the IRS and its shareholders file their K-1s with their individual tax returns.

If you are a one-person S corp, there may be fewer downsides, but when you have multiple people involved, managing it gets much more complex. Keeping up the stock ledger can get complicated when someone buys or sells their share of stock, for example.

On the other hand, if you're trying to raise funds and go public, an S corp is the way to go.

C Corporation

Although I can't quite imagine a situation when I would suggest that a real estate investor client set up a C corporation, it is an option. C corporations, or C corps, which are primarily for larger multinational enterprises, enjoy limited liability but are taxed at the corporate rate, rather than at the individual shareholder's tax rate.

The biggest difference with a C corp is that it is not a pass-through entity. There is double taxation. That means the profits and losses of the corporation do not pass through to the shareholders; the company pays taxes on what it earns. Then shareholders pay tax on the dividends the corporation pays out.

When setting up a C corp, you must file a Charter with the Secretary of State in your state. Similar to the LLC's Articles of Incorporation or Organization, the Charter sets forth basic information about the company, including how many shares the company is authorized to issue.

Where LLCs have operating agreements, C corps have by-laws, though corporations also use resolutions to announce decisions made by the shareholders or its board of directors.

But for a new real estate investor, I can't imagine when a C corporation would be the best choice to use for their new entity. There is rarely a benefit that would lead someone to use this type of business structure.

Trust

Trusts typically aren't used for real estate purchases, at least at the outset, unless we're talking about celebrities or family dynasties with enormous wealth. In Nashville, for example, a lot of the music stars hold their real estate in trusts. But the typical real estate investor isn't likely to go this route. It's almost counter-productive to put your real estate holdings into an entity that you can't then control. But let me explain briefly how trusts work.

Although there are several forms of trusts, I'm going to categorize them into two major categories: revocable and irrevocable.

Revocable trusts are those that the person who created the trust, also called the Grantor—which would be you—can control. It is included in your estate. Revocable trusts offer few protections.

Irrevocable trusts are those that you do not control; you assign ownership of your assets to the trust, including any properties you've purchased. Since the property is then no longer in your name, you cannot be liable for anything that happens related to it. Great for protection, not so great for controlling your real estate portfolio.

I've made it simple, but entire books have been written about trusts and this area of law is a niche unto itself. Trusts are very effective tools for enjoying the benefits of asset protection and estate planning while you receive the payments from the profits contained within it.

Trusts file their own tax returns and the beneficiaries report any income from their trusts on their tax returns.

Partnership

A partnership is an agreement between at least two people to work together to make money together in a business. There are different types of partnerships, including general, limited, limited liability, and LLC partnerships. Partnerships in real estate are very common. Typically, they are used in syndication deals, where several people form a joint venture and pool their money to buy some real estate.

But there are different types of partners, depending on their level of involvement in the property selection and management.

General Partnership

In a general partnership, the partners manage the business together and each assumes responsibility for the partnership's debts. Unlike LLCs, which provide their members liability protection, a general partnership leaves personal assets at risk. The partners are also responsible for each other's actions.

Limited Partnership

Limited partnerships have both general and limited partners, where the limited partners are usually only investors, while the general partners own and operate the company and assume the liabilities for the partnership.

Limited Liability Partnership (LLP)

Limited liability partnerships protect the assets of the limited partners, who are not held liable for any debts of the partners. They also do not have responsibility for the actions of the other partners. However, in an LLP, there must be at least one general partner who takes full responsibility for the entity.

Since protections for general and limited partners vary from state to state, check yours before agreeing to establish or become part of an LLP.

Limited Liability Company Partnership (LLCP)

LLCPs can be, and usually are, taxed as partnerships. In most cases, the members cannot be sued for the business's actions or debts, although the members can be liable for the actions of other members.

I have a client who owns a construction company south of Nashville. His brother, who was also his business partner, passed away a couple of years ago and the deceased brother's children wanted his share of the business. The problem became complicated in that the men had set up the company as a partnership in the 1970s. The laws have changed quite a bit since then, however, and the partnership was also converted to an LLC a number of years ago. Even more complicated, the brothers kept amending the partnership agreement instead of replacing it with an operating agreement, which is what an LLC uses. So, was it a partnership or an LLC? We had to figure that out.

In order to sort out who got what, we had to walk through the statutes, decade by decade, and parse out who was entitled to what. Fortunately, partnership law is well settled and all the lawyers were able to agree that even though there was a formal LLC filed, the intention of the parties was to treat this as a partnership.

In the end, we simply treated it as a partnership and split the assets according to state law and the pay-out provisions of the *last* partnership agreement; there were about five iterations through the years. Sometimes, partnerships are the way to go because of their simplicity, however, you'll definitely want to have a partnership agreement if you do choose this route.

No matter what type of partnership you may decide to establish, always, always have a partnership agreement. Your state's Secretary of State office can confirm what kind of paperwork is required, and some states may not require you to file anything in order to set up a partnership. Still, you'll want to lay out in writing what you and your partners agree to regarding how your company will be run, and what should happen if one or more of you want out. That's what a partnership is for, to eliminate misunderstandings that can create chaos down the line.

None of the Above

There is no requirement that you set up a separate entity to hold your property. You can certainly opt to hold the property in your individual name, buy insurance, and be cautious. The problem is that not everyone else will be equally cautious. That includes tenants, visitors, contractors, and others. By holding the property in your name, you are at risk of losing your personal assets should someone sue you because of something that happened at one of your properties.

Protecting Your Investment

No matter what entity you choose to create to hold your real estate, there are additional steps you can and should take to protect all of your assets. Because if something happens with that new real estate you just bought, it can put everything else you own in jeopardy, too.

The first thing to get is property insurance, which we'll talk about in more detail in Chapter 3, as well as an umbrella policy and a business policy for your new business entity.

The second thing is to add conditions to your lease agreements that spell out what renters are permitted and not permitted to do on your property.

In a long-term rental, you'll have a lease, which you should have a lawyer draft. Don't try to do this on your own.

As part of that lease, make sure to include a list of prohibited acts that will violate the lease and subject the resident to immediate eviction. It should say something like, "These are prohibited acts that will violate your lease and will subject you to be evicted: Any criminal act, any drug use, any party over [so many] people." You don't want huge parties or behavior that could lead to injury.

In a short-term rental, where parties are much more likely to occur—in fact, some people rent a property specifically for a blow-out party—you'll need to present a more exhaustive list of prohibited acts, which might depend on the amenities at the property. You'll definitely want to prohibit activities such as drugs, parties, and fireworks, and require that guests use things within the house only for the purposes for which they were designed.

Clearly, there are a number of options when it comes to how you can hold your real estate. It should be a business decision, guided by advice from professionals, including your attorney and accountant. While the LLC is the choice of a majority of real estate investors today, that doesn't mean it's the right choice *for you*. Ask the people who are advising you for their recommendation based on your particular situation.

Key Takeaways

- Decide how long you want to hold a property before you buy. Are you expecting three to five years, or more like ten-plus? That will affect your investing strategy.

- Creating an LLC protects you from personal responsibility for your company's debts and liabilities, as well as claims from tenants.

- S corporations have similar benefits to LLCs, but operate differently.

- If you're partnering with others, decide if you should operate as a formal partnership, or if another entity structure would make more sense for you.

- Partnerships can be a great way to pool money from multiple people or organizations in order to invest in larger projects or properties.

CHAPTER 3

SETTING UP YOUR BUSINESS CORRECTLY

No matter how you view real estate investing—whether you see it as a side hustle, a wealth-building strategy, or a way to generate additional income for yourself—it's important to understand that, first and foremost, it's a business—a serious business with lots of money at stake. For that reason, you need to set your business up properly from the start. That means filing the necessary paperwork and paying for services that will keep your investments safe.

While I'm going to encourage you to rely on the advice of professionals in order to stay out of trouble, you also need to understand what you're asking them to do and why. Handing off tasks to an accountant or attorney without fully knowing why you need them to do what you're asking is dangerous for you. You need to understand your business so you can protect it, and you, from getting into trouble down the line.

There are several steps you need to take to get your real estate investing business up and running legally and effectively. Many steps are seemingly easy to take care of, though I will recommend that you at least have a professional check your work to be sure you won't have issues down the line.

To set your business up effectively, you'll want to have the following:

Employer Identification Number (EIN)

Every company needs to have an employer identification number (EIN), also called a "tax ID number," issued. An EIN is the business equivalent of a social security number. The good news is that it's totally free and easy to get.

To have yours assigned, go to the IRS website, or Google "How to get an EIN."

If you are unsure of how to respond to some of the questions, consider handing off this task to your accountant or attorney to be sure it is completed properly. Can you do it yourself? Absolutely. But it may not be in your best interest to do it yourself. The last thing you want to do is to fill out paperwork improperly and then have to correct it later.

Don't Hire Based on Price

While I recommend that you turn to a skilled attorney for counsel as you set up your real estate investment company and proceed to buy your first property, I want to caution you against hiring a lawyer based on price. You've heard the adage that "you get what you pay for," and this is certainly true with attorneys. Don't opt for a bargain basement online generalist attorney who may or may not know real estate in the area where you're buying properties. The advice you get may not help you achieve your goals. You want to hire an attorney with real estate and business law expertise.

In fact, that's exactly what happened with Joe, who is a real estate investor who put all of his properties in a trust. Now, you may recall in Chapter 2 that I told you there is no good reason to put your properties in a trust.

Joe came to me for help in changing his revocable trust "to get his properties out of his name." His proposed solution was to create a new, separate trust for the real estate.

I didn't understand what that would accomplish, so I asked his business attorney about the reason for taking the real estate out of the revocable trust, and he wasn't sure either.

My recommendation was to set up a parent LLC, which would be a holding company, and then another LLC owned by the parent, which would be specifically for his real estate. "That way, he can invest in other things, he can take investors, and it gives him both the control and liability protection he wants," I said.

So that's what we did. But it was much more expensive because the properties were already held in trust and had to be moved into a new LLC. It would have been better if Joe had asked his attorney how to achieve his objectives before forming the trust in the first place. He ended up spending more on attorney's fees than if he had asked for advice up front. Which is why that's my advice to you—talk to your lawyer before you get everything set up to avoid having to make expensive changes later.

Although the questions on the online EIN form are simple, if you misconstrue what you're being asked, you could misclassify your business. For example, you're asked on the first page what type of entity you have. Are you registering as an individual, an LLC, a corporation, a partnership, etc.? Be sure you know what kind of legal structure you elected before you start filling this out.

On the next page, you'll fill in information about yourself, as well as the reason you're requesting an EIN (which is usually because you've started a new business) and what type of business you're in. Real estate is an option, and you need to be clear about the type of real estate business you're running, whether it's construction, or you're a contractor, or an agent, or professional. There are nuances here you need to be sure about. If you're not, ask your attorney for guidance before you submit the form.

As soon as you have it, use your EIN in place of your social security number whenever completing paperwork related to your real estate holdings.

Business Bank Account

You'll also need a bank account for your business, to keep real estate and personal finances separate. Call or ask around to see which banks will set up business accounts for real estate investing, and which are the most convenient for you to access.

You'll probably need to go into a branch in person to set up the account, and you'll need to bring with you an ID, your EIN, your LLC documents or articles of incorporation, as well as anything else the bank wants to see.

Choosing a Bank

Some banks will not allow accounts for real estate investments, so it's important to confirm that you can use your account for that purpose before you set it up. I, personally, use three banks (see the Resources section for my contacts). Two are local banks, where everyone knows me and my wife by name, and where they're familiar with our holdings. The other is a publicly traded large bank, which is useful when we're buying properties outside of our local area. There's no wrong bank, so long as they will permit business bank accounts for real estate investments and you can get easy access to your funds when you need them.

State Tax Department Account

Now that you have your company's EIN and a business bank account, you need to go online to your state's tax department, also called the Department of Revenue in some states, and set up an account there for online tax payments. You'll link your business bank account to it so that you can immediately pay any taxes owed that way.

Business License

Some counties require a business license for real estate investing companies, so you'll want to check to see if one is required where you've established your company. Call your attorney to ask whether one is needed, either locally or in the county where your property is situated.

After setting up the required state and federal business and tax accounts, there are other expenses for you to include in your budget. Not all will apply to your specific situation, but you'll want to allocate funds to more than cover those that do. This is all part of running a real estate investing business.

Insurance

The purpose of insurance is to protect your assets in case of damage. That damage could be due to frozen pipes that burst, for example, or the flooding of the nearby creek, or a tenant causing a grease fire on the stovetop. You can't anticipate what crisis might occur, but you can certainly protect yourself from huge repair expenses by purchasing insurance.

The insurance policies you will want to buy include:

- Business insurance for your real estate company, in the form of a general liability policy, which covers routine business liabilities and losses for all your back-office equipment and technology you will need to manage your property/properties
- Homeowner's policy on the dwelling and its replacement value

I recommend calling your insurance agent for any current policies you have, to ask what kind of coverage you can get. Not all insurance companies cover real estate investment firms, so you may need to ask around.

My wife and I own a small, single-family house in Chattanooga, Tenn. Being in the South, we do get tornadoes from time to time. However, since Chattanooga is encircled by mountains—Signal Mountain, Lookout Mountain, and Missionary Ridge—I cannot remember there ever having been a tornado where this particular property is located.

Notice I didn't say there had "never" been a tornado. It was certainly within the realm of possibilities.

Of course, a couple of years ago, a tornado hit Chattanooga and knocked a tree onto the house. Thank goodness our tenant was uninjured and the house could be repaired. We called our insurance agent, made the claim, and repaired the roof. If we had not had insurance, this repair would have cost $20,000 out of pocket for the roof repair and tree removal.

Learn from my experience, don't cheap out on insurance coverage. Sure, shop rates, but get full coverage. You only need it when you need it.

Property Taxes

Every piece of property you buy will have property taxes associated with it. Depending on where it is located, you may actually have more than one taxing authority on the property, such as the city and county, or village and town, simultaneously. I mention this so you can budget accordingly.

The local tax authorities will mail your tax bills. We just paid our Chattanooga and Knoxville taxes, and are awaiting bills for our properties in Montana and Gatlinburg. But the bills weren't a surprise. You can know what to expect by looking at last year's taxes, which are available in the tax records. Moreover, if you are looking to buy a property, the previous year's tax records are typically listed in the property description on MLS or on Realtor.com.

To ensure you have the funds available to pay taxes when they come due, you'll want to set aside funds from each month's rent to cover 1/12th of the taxes that will be owed. Look at tax records for each property you own to understand what the current annual taxes are, so you can divide by twelve to calculate the monthly obligation.

Homeowner's Association (HOA) Fees

HOA fees cover the cost to keep the property (and common areas) functioning and well-maintained, and ensure that all properties in the neighborhood are also well-kept. They help preserve your investment's value. However, higher HOA fees can make properties less appealing to buyers, which is an issue if you're hoping to quickly renovate and flip a particular property.

Not all properties are subject to HOA fees, however. You'll want to ask before you commit to a purchase. Depending on a property's amenities, some HOA fees end up being higher than your monthly mortgage. For example, if a property is within a gated or a town-house community with a swimming pool, tennis courts, sauna, and playground, you should expect to chip in more for upkeep than if the property is a condo in a high-rise with a lobby. Higher HOA fees can make it very difficult to earn any income, because they are an added expense for which you have to budget.

And not all townhouses, condos, or communities require them. Personally, I would look for a property that doesn't have a monthly fee.

Repairs and Maintenance

Any property, including newly constructed buildings, will need maintenance at some point. Some require seasonal maintenance, such as cleaning out leaf-filled gutters each fall or lawn aeration each spring, while others have larger issues that emerge, such as cleaning out a septic tank, relocating rodents or insects, or refinishing hardwood floors.

Although you don't personally have to attend to your property's maintenance needs, you'll need to set aside funds to pay professionals to address them if you aren't qualified or interested. Ignoring problems when they arise will only cause larger issues for tenants or buyers, which will cost you more money. Take care of maintenance when it is needed, rather than deferring it.

Property Management Fees

If your investing goal is to buy properties to rent out, whether on a short-term or long-term basis, you may opt to hire a property management firm. These firms can be essential in renting out and managing your properties, and make more sense the larger your portfolio of properties grows.

Fees for property management can range from as little as 3%, which is on the low side, to as much as 55%, at the top of the market. The percentage of the rent that the firm requires will depend on the type of real estate, its location, and the class of property.

It's important that you're aware of these fees before you commit to buying a property and hiring a firm, because they can make or break your profitability. Short-term rental firms often charge above 15% for their services, while long-term rental management companies are more likely to charge less than 15% of the rent.

On the commercial side, commercial real estate management fees vary greatly, depending on the services provided, the size of the property, the type of property, and its location.

Legal Fees

You're going to want a good lawyer to advise you on many aspects of real estate investing and ownership. Look for an attorney or a firm that understands your goals and can help you achieve them. I'm a lawyer and I pay other lawyers regularly for matters that arise from my owning real estate. Do your homework to find a skilled lawyer who can keep you out of trouble and advise you on the best ways to get out of trouble when you're dragged into it.

There are a number of areas where you'll want a pro to advise you, including:

- Setting up your business structure, as mentioned in Chapter 2
- Maintaining your corporate form
- Evictions
- Standard operating procedures

Setting up your business structure

If you haven't already decided which legal entity to use in setting up your LLC, S corp, partnership, or trust, now is a good time to look for an attorney or law firm that is well-versed in real estate. Your attorney can explain the various fees associated with each entity, how to maintain it, the tax implications of each choice, and how best to operate it.

Maintaining your corporate form

Once your company has been set up, you'll want a lawyer to help keep your company in good standing with your state, by documenting your corporate actions, filing appropriate licensures, and guiding you in how to maintain the corporate veil that protects you from liability related to your property. Lawyers can also help keep your minute book up-to-date, reflecting the latest in the ever-changing requirements of the law.

Evictions

At some point in your real estate investing journey, you will need to evict someone. It's inevitable, so expect it. Maybe your renter hasn't paid, maybe they've moved in fifteen of their fraternity buddies without permission, or perhaps they've violated noise ordinances which have breached their lease with you. Whatever the reason is for eviction, it's best to turn the situation over to a lawyer to handle to ensure you're proceeding lawfully.

In some states, lawyers are required to represent corporate entities in such matters. Even if you aren't required to use one, it will be in your best interest to have a knowledgeable lawyer helping you to navigate the eviction process, to help protect you from a misstep that could cost you time or money.

Advice

Most importantly, lawyers can be your sounding board as problems and opportunities arise. They can give you feedback and recommendations for how to address situations, providing a legal perspective that you otherwise would not have spotted. I often discuss legal and business issues with other lawyers because no one has seen it all and can immediately spot the best course of action. It's always a good idea to speak with someone who has likely dealt with the situation you're facing multiple times, whereas it's only your first.

The fees your lawyer charges will be well worth the peace of mind that accompanies the bill.

Key Takeaways

- Rely on advice from professionals when setting up your business, rather than friends or family. You'll avoid trouble later by listening to paid experts.
- Don't hire an attorney based on price, hire based on experience—preferably real estate and/or real estate investing.
- Talk to your lawyer before you finalize your business structure, in order to avoid expensive changes later.

- Don't choose the most convenient bank for your business accounts, but do your research and compare policies, interest rates, and mortgage processes first.
- Buy insurance policies on your business and the properties you own.

CHAPTER 4

───⟨∾⟩───

BUILDING YOUR TEAM

B ecoming a successful real estate investor requires a team of professionals to support and guide your business's growth. As with
anything, when you start a new venture, you don't know what you
don't know. Making decisions is difficult because you don't have
enough experience or expertise to evaluate all your options. This is
why surrounding yourself with experienced, knowledgeable, ethical
professionals is critical. They can help you find properties, value
them, finance them, renovate them, rent them, clean and maintain
them, protect them, and manage your money.

Easier said than done, of course. Even when you know what skills
you need, finding talented, hard-working advisors can be challenging.
However, when you know what you need your team to accomplish
for you, and the tasks they'll be responsible for, you can start your
search by asking for recommendations from your growing network
of fellow investors.

Nearly every businessowner should have the following people or
professional firms on speed dial, to help you make the best decisions
possible for your properties and your long-term goals. These include:

Bookkeeper

Before you can hand over your numbers to your accountant to
determine what you owe or don't owe the IRS, you first could use

the services of a bookkeeper. Some accounting firms employ book-keepers who organize all your money categories, while smaller ones may not. Ask around to see who does a good job of getting finances organized and regularly recorded and tracked.

Bookkeepers basically track the cash inflow and outflow on each property. Tracking them is important because, for example, expenses under $2,500 can be written off in a year, whereas larger expenses, over $2,500, have to be capitalized and taken as a deduction over several years. You need a bookkeeper paying attention to all of your expenses and then categorizing them according to how quickly they can be deducted.

Your bookkeeper can also tell you how each house is performing. Think of it like a stock, and it either performs or it doesn't. If it's costing too much money, you need to get rid of it. And your book-keeper can make you aware of which of your assets, your properties, are consistently underperforming so that you can decide how to proceed. But you want a bookkeeper who has real estate expertise and not a general bookkeeper.

Most accountants have connections to good bookkeepers, so ask yours who specializes in real estate bookkeeping, and who they recommend.

Meet in Person

I always find it helpful to sit across from someone you're thinking of hiring, whether that person is a bookkeeper, accountant, banker, or attorney. I think meeting in person can provide a lot more information about them and how they operate than a phone call, so I encourage you to interview potential team members face-to-face. Some may charge a consultation fee for doing that, and I don't think that's unreasonable, but it could save you a lot of time and trouble down the line.

Accountant

I have used the largest national accounting firms, the local 800-pound gorilla, as well as the local mom-and-pop shop. You might be surprised to know that the winning player for me was the mom-and-pop operation. The large national firm overlooked a $50,000 payment I had already made to the IRS and failed to file my self-employment tax, which created more work, and the regional accounting firm made multiple errors on my return and then had the gall to send me a $14,000 bill for services. I needed an accountant who knew the ins and outs of real estate taxation, and the one I found is in a smaller firm; she knows her stuff.

My accountant loves to geek out on tax talk. She gets into the details that CPAs and tax lawyers discuss at tax conferences. Once she understood how things were structured within my real estate investing business, we discussed our larger goals for growth and income, and we bounced ideas back and forth to find a path forward that worked for all of us, in terms of creating tax losses.

Since I am self-employed and my wife is not, it is paramount that we create tax losses so that we can continue to grow our portfolio. If this sounds counterintuitive, think of it this way: If you could take the money you'd have to pay the IRS for taxes owed and reduce it through losses you take on your real estate, you'd have funds you could instead use to buy other properties. By purchasing additional properties, we are buying more deductions, especially depreciation. It is important to understand, however, that tax losses don't mean that you are not cash positive. This is a distinction your team can help you understand.

Tax losses are created by deductions available to you from the asset. Your accountant and bookkeeper will be your go-to team members to help you with tax losses.

For me and my wife, our goals are long term and we need an accountant who understands our goal and how to get there. My accountant makes it her mission to comb the tax code to make sure we are taking advantage of everything we can. The key is that she is a tax accountant who knows real estate.

This does not mean that I didn't switch up my accounting firms a few times before finding her, however. It took time, but once you find the right fit for you, things move much more efficiently.

Lawyer

As I discussed in the previous chapter, having a good lawyer who understands business, real estate, and taxes is paramount. Not only does your lawyer need to understand your business, that lawyer needs to understand your industry. From those two perspectives, it benefits you if your lawyer can speak fluently with your accountant. Your time needs to be spent finding deals and managing your real estate goals, and your professional advisors need to take the legal and accounting off the table for you, so you can focus on what makes you money—real estate investing.

The confluence of real estate, taxes, and business law is not unusual. Most business attorneys are going to have touched both taxes and real estate. However, make sure any lawyer you talk to has a solid understanding of what you want. You want a lawyer who can help you evaluate a deal, help you draft contracts, negotiate them, and have a very firm grasp on real estate investing, litigation, and transactions. I do not recommend that you engage a budget lawyer or generalist who can put your money and properties at risk because they don't understand the nuances of real estate investing.

Look at Attorney Ratings

Attorneys are rated by third-party rating companies, such as Martindale-Hubbell, which is used to grade attorneys as either A, B, or C. Today, they rate attorneys as either AV Preeminent (the highest rating), Distinguished, or Notable. *Super Lawyers* magazine, which has editions in various regions around the country, only includes attorneys who have been nominated by at least five of their peers. These ratings can be a starting point for at least finding a reputable attorney. You'll need to decide for yourself if they're a good fit for your business and personality, however.

Banker

The right banker at the right bank is a make-or-break player; those are two factors for you to consider (whether the bank provides the services you need and how well your banking representative can represent your best interests). For example, if you anticipate quickly owning more than ten properties, you may need to identify a bank that provides commercial financing in addition to personal. Once you own more than ten properties, you won't qualify for a personal mortgage, and it's useful not to have to start from scratch in building a new relationship with a commercial banker somewhere else. So, think ahead about what you might need from a bank, to help you choose one that can grow with your business. For example, when you amass a portfolio of up to ten properties, you may want to cross-collateralize the properties to leverage the aggregate equity you've built up in order to buy more properties. A sophisticated banker and bank can help you do this. Sometimes the smaller banks cannot stomach that kind of sophistication in real estate investing.

You need a relationship banker who understands what you are trying to achieve, will help guide you and your projects to get there, and makes your life easier. Get recommendations from friends, colleagues, and other investors. Banks make money on you but really good bankers help you make multiples of that spent money back. A great banker will also open doors for you through introductions to people with whom you might have a great synergy. Building the right team also builds a great network.

Insurance Agent

If you are buying real estate, or just running a business, you need to have a good insurance agent. They understand your company's needs and are the ones you call when things go south.

All of my insurance is with one agent. That agent, in turn, has not only told me about deals, but he has also connected me with possible deal makers that have the potential to become a deal. They are plugged in to your business community and can become your most important call if something happens at one of your properties. Insurance agents can also make you aware of other financial products that will provide cash reserves that grow tax-free and provide you with security. Before you roll your eyes about sitting down with an insurance agent, go have a conversation; you might be surprised what you learn from them.

Property Manager

Do you take the 11:00 P.M. phone call about a clogged toilet? I don't and I won't. Property managers are buffers between tenants and owners that can save you time and money, while also keeping an eye on how tenants are treating your property. They are good stewards of your real estate and money.

Good property managers are also problem-solvers, and make sure elevators work, the landscaping is clean, and the facilities are operational. They also usually don't get paid unless the rent gets paid, so they are incentivized to make sure everything is in working order.

When you're just getting started, you may decide to be your own property manager, and that's fine. But if you buy properties that are more than an hour's drive away, I'd find a property manager right away. You don't have the time to be driving at least two hours round-trip to do what needs to be done. Instead, hire a reputable property manager who can save you that time. This will save you money in the long run.

I highly recommend interviewing any property manager in person, so that you can ask questions about how they operate. Treat them like a potential employee and find out what their response time is, how many employees they have to service all their properties, and ask for references, too, to confirm what they're telling you.

We have interviewed and used a lot of property managers, some who were terrific and others who were downright negligent. We recently fired a property manager after a history of nickel-and-diming us and spending money we had not authorized them to spend. But the kicker was that they received a tenant's notice to leave and had assumed the tenant left. But I guess no one bothered to check, and he came back and didn't tell anyone. It wasn't until our real estate agent was showing the property that they discovered someone was living there. The property manager needs to stay on top of those types of things, change locks, etc.

STR or LTR Agent

Property managers responsible for renting out your units will either specialize in short-term rentals, as with Airbnb, or long-term rentals, meaning more like an annual lease. So, you need to know what type of rental you're going after before you hire a property manager. And keep in mind that the compensation structure is also different depending on which type of rentals they handle. STR property managers typically make around 20% of the rental amount, while LTR is more like 8% to 10%. But the more doors you get under management with the same firm, the more you can negotiate the fee.

Handyman

Over the course of a property's life, it is going to need to have routine maintenance performed. Small projects to large, a good maintenance provider helps keep the property in good shape. A healthy property means happy tenants, and you know the rest. From handymen who can tackle a simple task like repairing a window, to full-service maintenance providers, this member of your team is necessary.

Ask for references and to see examples of their work.

Although we have a property manager, sometimes a handyman can be much more cost-effective, even on larger tasks. A case-in-point is that we recently had an air conditioning unit go out in one of our properties in Knoxville, so the property manager sent his employee out and they quoted around $10,000 to replace it. That sounded high to me, so I tracked down an AC repairman through our real estate agent and asked him to give us a second opinion. He looked at it and told us it was an $800 repair. He ordered the part and fixed it, saving us many thousands of dollars. So, it can often pay to have a handyman take a look at problems that come up.

Real Estate Agent

I've included real estate agents toward the end of this chapter because you don't always need one. Yes, agents can be instrumental in finding out about properties and handling the purchase of them, but you don't necessarily have to have a single agent on speed dial. Because you may decide to invest in geographic areas where they don't operate, such as if you're looking out of town or even out of state, you should retain a real estate agent who works in the geographic region where the property is located. This is because your local agent likely doesn't know much about the market 500 miles away.

For example, when we bought our property in Montana, we weren't working with anyone in particular, so we called the listing agent who was representing the property. Dealing directly with that agent did two things for us: 1) It gave us an inside track to hearing what the buyer was really willing to accept and 2) it gave us a certain amount of leverage because the listing agent was going to earn the whole commission on the deal and not have to split it with anyone and assumedly, she was very motivated to help us close that deal. (Although the typical sales commission is 6%, when an agent represents both buyer and seller, some are willing to knock it down to 5%, which the seller is paying.)

For that reason, when we're looking to buy outside of our area, we try to use the agent who has listed the property as our agent. It makes the whole process smoother.

In Knoxville, we have an agent who is worth his weight in gold. He is phenomenal. He brings us deals, he turns things around fast, and since he's a builder, he helps spot problem areas that may need to be corrected. I go to him first when we're looking in Knoxville.

However, you don't have to have an agent. A case-in-point is a recent situation we dealt with where we were under a 1031 exchange, meaning we needed to identify within 45 days which properties we would be purchasing and had 180 days to close on that purchase. We had been scouring the listings, trying to find a property to buy, and they just were not out there. So, I called a client who is a real estate investor and asked if he might want to offload any properties. He told us, "Yes, I have eighteen properties out in Brownsville and I'd sell you one for whatever it appraises for." He had bought them for next to nothing, so he knew he was going to profit at whatever the appraisal said. He wrote up the contract and we bought it, without an agent. That happens a lot between investors.

The list of individuals I suggest having on your team is not exhaustive, but it is a good place to start. Once you have a good team, the synergies will begin playing off each other and deals will happen more frequently. More deals mean more success. Do not be afraid to kiss some frogs. Your team is mission critical to your success.

Key Takeaways

- Hire a bookkeeper with real estate expertise, not just a general business bookkeeper.
- Meet anyone you are thinking of hiring in person. There is so much you can tell by being in their presence that you may miss on a telephone or Zoom call.
- Don't rule out local accountants, they are sometimes more thorough and knowledgeable than the bigger firms.
- You don't always need a real estate agent to buy properties, but they can turn out to be valuable connections that can lead to more deals for you.

CHAPTER 5

―∽―

FINDING PROPERTIES

All of this information on running a real estate investment business is great in concept, but it's completely useless to you unless and until you find a property to purchase. The combination of the rise of the popularity of Airbnb, the pandemic push into the suburbs for more living space, and low mortgage rates have resulted in exponential price increases on residential properties in the early 2020s. Are there properties available today? Yes. Are you likely to get a bargain deal? Not so much. But don't let that stop you. You don't need a bargain to make a real estate investment purchase make sense.

It all comes down to why you're investing in real estate to begin with. What's your goal? Income? Wealth building? New career? Inflation hedge?

That answer will guide the types of properties you should be looking for, and how sensitive you can be on purchase price.

Starting Out

If you're just getting started and don't have much experience in looking for real estate, because maybe the only property you've bought is your first home, there are some easy-to-use websites and apps that list the majority of single-family and multifamily properties currently on the market. Although there are probably more than a dozen real estate search sites, these four are the ones I use regularly:

- Multiple Listing Service (MLS)
- Realtor
- Redfin
- Zillow

Using these online platforms allows you to quickly see what properties are available, as well as the ones that have recently sold. The information isn't always the most up-to-date, however, and even if a home sale is pending, it may be contingent and the seller may be open to other offers, or it may say, "Accepting back-up offers." Not all platforms will show that level of detail, however.

You can also look into court-ordered tax auctions, or tax sales. Every county that takes ownership of homes due to lack of property tax payments has a process for reselling those units. Find out what that entails in your county. In some, the houses are auctioned off to cash buyers once a month on the front steps of the county courthouse. Others have, instead, partnered with auction houses or companies to handle that process.

During the auction, you can bid on properties of interest to you. Make sure you know what the tax lien amount is, so you can factor it into how much you're willing to spend, in total, for a property.

When you win such a tax auction, it's not as easy as simply taking possession of the property once you pay your bid amount and any taxes owed. Instead, you first need to complete the statutory period of waiting, which is usually a year. During that time, the original owner has had the chance to "redeem" the property by paying whatever you paid for it, plus the interest that has accrued during that period. You will want to check your state's law to confirm. If that does not occur, you essentially have to foreclose on the property to make it yours.

The advantage of tax auctions is that you may be able to buy a property for well under market value. That's important if your goal is to flip it, or to renovate it and then turn around and resell it fast. It's also good news if you're still building up your investment account and are trying to buy more economical homes.

Although real estate platforms and apps may be easy to use, they aren't necessarily your best source of property information. That title goes to local real estate agents.

My preferred way of scouting for properties is to call an agent I've used in the area and ask, "Hey, do you have any off-market deals or pocket listings?"

Pocket Listing

A pocket listing is a property listing that the listing agent does not post in the multiple listing system (MLS) and is expected to sell through their own channels. The advantage of pocket listings to buyers is that there may be less competition for it since it hasn't been publicly broadcast to the market.

The biggest advantage of getting an off-market deal (meaning one that is not on the public MLS) is there are no real estate agencies involved. The agent who has the pocket listing for an off-market deal typically represents both seller and buyer in the deal. They still are paid a commission, however, whether or not the property was ever publicly listed for sale.

You could also ask agents, "Hey, do you have any investors who might be looking to sell any of their properties?" Sometimes real estate investors would consider selling off some of their portfolio and are open to a sale if the right deal comes along. All it takes is asking some questions.

There is no such thing as a stupid question in real estate, so don't be afraid to ask. The field is so big and so complex that you are not expected to have all the answers, or even to easily uncover them. Just keep learning and asking in order to make progress.

My client, Jeff, lives in New York and went under contract for the purchase of a property here in Tennessee in 2020. However, Jeff decided that he didn't want to go through with the purchase. He wanted to get out of the contract and was willing to lose his $3,500 earnest money deposit to do so. He called me for help.

I was able to discuss his options with him and suggested that he allow me a few hours to see what I could come up with. I started by calling my personal real estate agent in the area, Darin Cunningham. In three hours, Darin had me an offer to buy that property for a $90,000 profit with a 21-day close, post my client's closing. By tapping into his investor network, Darin knew who to pitch the offer to and the deal was struck that evening. Jeff would never have to make a payment on the mortgage and would walk away with a $90,000 profit without ever doing anything.

The moral of the story? It pays to ask members of your team for help.

Although there is no right or wrong way to find a property, I've found that tapping into my network is the most efficient way to go when I'm looking to buy. When you're starting out, you may not have your own network, so you need to build one. One good way is to attend local Meetups of real estate investors. BiggerPockets sponsors them in many cities, but there are likely others, too, including Facebook groups, so research where your closest real estate investor event is and check it out. I started my own real estate group on Facebook, called Real Estate Investing for All. I post almost daily about investing in real estate and encourage people in the group to connect, talk, and get to know each other. Most of my personal network contacts are on this page.

Meetup is another platform for finding in-person investor get-togethers, which can be a great way to expand your own network.

A Targeted Search

Real estate agents are great starting points to find out what might be available, but if you know specific properties you'd like to own, you can try a different strategy. It's called a postcard campaign, which some agents use, and which involves mailing postcards to homeowners asking if they'd be interested in selling their property. To do that you do need to drive through an area, note the addresses you're interested in, look up who owns it, and then mail out letters or postcards asking if they would entertain an offer. There's no guarantee that you'll get a response, but postcards or letters can be a fairly easy way to connect with property owners to see if they'd sell.

Mailing postcards to specific addresses is a more targeted approach to finding properties than picking up the phone or texting an agent out of the blue to see if they know anyone who might be looking to sell.

Doors versus Properties

Real estate investors generally talk about their property holdings in terms of "doors," rather than number of homes or properties. Doors refer to the number of units you own. A duplex, for example, has two doors, because it is two separate properties. You are receiving two rent checks from that. A four-apartment multifamily property consists of four doors. So, you might own two properties but have ten doors. Always talk in terms of the doors you own.

The Time to Buy is Now

The saying, "He who hesitates is lost," applies to real estate investing. Meaning, if you wait too long, you will miss out on opportunities, whether we're talking about booking a vacation rental, ordering a hot toy for your child, or buying a property in a busy market.

The best time to buy a property is today. Not tomorrow or next month, but today.

Will mortgage interest rates go up? It's quite likely, yes. Should that stop you from investing? Absolutely not.

The reason you should invest now is that the mortgage interest rate you lock in won't have any effect on the rent or lease rate you're able to collect from tenants. If you're able to rent your property for a profitable amount, at the current interest rate, stop worrying about it. If you've run the numbers and you know your mortgage payment based on current interest rates, and you also know that you can rent your property for at least 1% of the property's purchase price each month, the bank's interest rate is immaterial. It's not something you need to worry about.

For example, if you buy a property for, say, $250,000, with a mortgage of $200,000, and can rent it for $2,000/week, or $8,000/month on Airbnb, you are more than covering your mortgage payment, taxes, and expenses. That's true whether your mortgage rate is 3%, 4%, or 5%. Does it matter much that your associated monthly mortgage payment is $843, $955, or $1,074 (which are the amounts owed at each interest rate)? No, it really doesn't. With those numbers, you're still able to earn a healthy profit, even at higher interest rates.

So, stop using rising interest rates as the excuse that keeps you from jumping into the market. It shouldn't be a factor in your decision-making. This is so because even as interest rates may rise, so too will the value of many investments. Five years from now, I like to tell my clients, it's very likely that any property you currently own will be worth more than it is today.

Now, will mortgage interest rates affect how much you can qualify for? Yes. But what I'm trying to tell you is the interest rate does not determine whether a property is a good investment.

How to Find the "Right" Property

I had a good friend stay with us over the holidays. He has some money set aside for investments, and he kept asking Dawn and me how we find the right properties.

Although the answer depends on you and your goals, my wife and I answered in unison: "Run the numbers." He laughed at hearing our response in stereo and then asked: "What does that mean?"

We tried to explain that it depends on the investor and what that investor wants from the property.

For example, if his plan as an investor is to buy a property, have it pay for itself, and sell that property in a few years for a tidy profit, then that's one set of factors. And in that case, the monthly profit is not as important for that investor, *as long as* the property pays for itself.

On the other hand, if he needs the money to subsidize his income and help pay for his current lifestyle, then the numbers change. The monthly profit is the largest consideration in that scenario because cash flow is the goal. And that will likely entail looking for an entirely different property.

Let's look at the two main ways rental properties will generate revenue for the investor.

Long-Term Rentals (LTRs)

For LTRs, meaning residents who intend to stay a year or more, the websites I mentioned earlier—such as Realtor.com, Zillow, and the local area Multiple Listing Service (MLS)—are good places to *start* your search. These online search engines allow you to take the temperature of the area you are interested in, to see how much demand there is, what typical price points are, how safe it is, and whether it's a neighborhood in transition or if it's going downhill. You can filter your property searches by square footage, acreage, bedrooms, bathrooms, and community statistics for crime, schools, flood zone, and other criteria that property owners and renters take into account for renting.

Once you have conducted your online search, drive the area. Get a feel for the neighborhoods. Check out the landmarks and amenities. Educate yourself on the rents for that neighborhood by calling your real estate agent and asking; they should be able to relatively quickly tell you the average rents in the area. You can also check out Rentometer, which is pretty accurate; there is a free version and a paid version.

While the listing services will have properties for sale, those properties are for sale at retail prices. Depending on the economy in that market, retail purchases may not yield the returns you seek; meaning, there is a chance you will overpay at retail prices, which is why I encourage you to turn to networking to uncover properties that aren't currently on the market, such as through a pocket listing, or by proactively asking homeowners if they'd consider selling, or calling fellow investors. Other investors tend to be the best resource for investors.

Short-Term Rentals (STRs)

The first place to look for STRs is with property managers. This past holiday season, as we were sitting around having a glass of wine with our friend, my wife received a text message from our property manager for one of our STRs. He had come across an off-market deal—a property that had not been listed for sale but was going to be listed shortly. He knew we were in the market for another STR and called us first to learn if we might be interested.

We went under contract a few hours later. That's the value of your network.

Another place to find STRs would be local real estate agents with investor-clients. Agents often know if their clients are willing to sell their investments and have quick access to the rent-rolls—monthly revenue reports for the property—and the maintenance reports for expenditures the owners have made to maintain the property.

Finding Renters

Two of the leading online property management tools, Buildium and TurboTenant, have a built-in feature to share any of your property listings with a wide range of rental sites. Once you type up your property description and upload it to Buildium or TurboTenant, you can then syndicate where it is shown, meaning disseminate it to multiple websites for renters. Just some of the sites include Apartments.com, ApartmentList, Lovely, Zillow, Zumper, Dwellsy, and you can even list it on Craigslist. Although hired property managers are generally responsible for advertising and renting properties, if you're self-managing, one of these tools can serve as your rental agent.

Fix and Flips and BRRRRs

If you're not looking for a rental property, but something to buy, renovate, and resell, driving the area is the best way to start. It's not uncommon for a potential investment property to be unlisted and just sitting. Driving the area is the best way to see what is going on and to notice what's not moving.

Also, tap into your network of other investors. You might be surprised to hear that other investors know about lots of other opportunities that they aren't interested in themselves but that might be perfect for you.

This particular investment model can move more quickly if you're already working closely with a good banker and real estate agent. Both of those team members have knowledge of deals gone wrong, foreclosures, investors looking to offload properties, and information that is otherwise not generally known. You'll also need them to make any deals happen.

How Agents Can Help You

If you're looking to purchase property outside your local area, where you may not know anyone or have a real estate agent working for you, don't be afraid to pick up the phone and call the listing agent. They'll be happy to show you the property and work with you because then they can get the commission on both sides of the deal.

In these situations, where the agent is representing both buyer and seller, the commission is typically reduced from 6% to 5% or 4%. Using the same agent that the seller is using neutralizes the agent for advocating for either side. This typically fosters cooperation from all parties.

Defining Your Target Area

Although the time may be right to buy, assuming you have the money available to invest, not every location is the right area to buy in. You need to look for pockets of affordability that are generally found in the bedroom communities outside major metropolitan areas. What I mean is that you may not be able to get the numbers to work on a property in, say, downtown Atlanta, Chicago, or San Diego, but if you draw a circle radius around a city of twenty-five miles, you will likely strike gold. Outside of those major cities, you can often find an LTR for half the price of what downtown properties are selling for.

Bedroom communities are the suburban towns and smaller cities where most downtown workers go home to at night. There, you'll typically find lower housing costs, a lower cost of living overall, but with the major amenities you want, like grocery stores, department stores, and Starbucks.

Right now, for example, the housing costs in downtown Nashville are sky-high. It's difficult to find affordable housing of any kind there, including investment properties. The numbers just don't work. But if you look twenty or twenty-five miles outside of Nashville, you'll find towns that are more affordable, and where the real estate values are still climbing. You have a chance of getting into a reasonably priced property there, where it will also appreciate over the next few years. Our home outside Nashville has more than doubled in the last five years, for example.

If you have the choice between a single-family home and a multifamily property for a long-term rental, I would encourage you to consider the multifamily. I would rather have two rents coming out of one property, such as with a duplex, than a single payment. It's less risky that way, particularly if one tenant starts having money problems, for example. So, I like a duplex more than a single-family home, and a triplex or quadplex more than a duplex. Small multifamily properties are my preference.

If you're planning on doing short-term rentals, it's important that you check out any zoning restrictions within your municipality. Some towns and counties are cracking down on STRs and a homeowner's ability to rent their home on a short-term basis based on poor experiences with renters who throw loud parties or who simply aren't good neighbors during their stay. Or, if you're looking at a condo or townhouse as your investment, ask if the homeowner's association (HOA) permits such rentals; it's usually spelled out in the HOA guidelines.

You'll generally have an easier time finding STR opportunities in vacation or tourist areas. We like Gatlinburg, Tenn., for example, because people love to come into town to visit Dollywood, which is in nearby Pigeon Forge. No one lives full-time in Gatlinburg, it seems, and we've had no problem renting our properties there.

We currently have two cabins in Gatlinburg, with a goal of owning a total of ten eventually. We're being careful about our purchases because we want each property to cash flow 10% of the purchase price per year. So, if we buy a $500,000 property, we want to be able to make $50,000/year on it. It needs to be able to pay for itself.

Of course, that doesn't mean that we'd be able to pocket that whole $50,000 because we still need to use some of the money to pay the mortgage, the 20% management fee, maintenance, and utilities. Anything above that is profit.

What to Expect at Closing

If you've never been to a closing, you may be imagining a stressful process where your ability to own a property hangs in the balance. But it's not like that at all.

In fact, a closing is truly where you sign document after document under the watchful eye of a closing attorney, notary, or paralegal. It's not stressful, though your hand may cramp after signing your name twenty or more times! But, you already have the property, and this is simply when the paperwork is filed.

By law, you have to have seen a few of those documents before you arrive at the title attorney's office—documents like the closing statement and the interest rate declaration. Others you'll be seeing for the first time, like the personal guarantee, promising you'll repay the loan, the release of funds, and maybe some resolutions if you're holding the property in an LLC.

After twenty minutes or so, you're all done. Although you used to have to bring cash to the closing, it's possible that won't be necessary. You can have money transferred from your account to wherever it needs to go, so that no checks are necessary. Be sure to confirm that before you show up, however.

Whether you're after an LTR or STR, you will want to make sure it is cash flow positive—that it's generating sufficient rents to cover the mortgage and all of the associated expenses. Most properties that are being sold as a rental, either short-term or long-term, have a payment history that you should ask the seller about examining before you buy it. Make sure it makes sense for you.

That doesn't mean a small amount of rent will automatically knock a property out of contention, however, because there could be legitimate reasons the rent collected has been low. For example, did the owner use the property themselves during the prime season and not rent it out then? Did they not use a property management firm that would have brought in renters? Find out the story behind that rent amount, whatever it is.

Always be looking for properties that could be smart investments. Go for drives in nearby communities to see what's available. Check out neighborhoods while you're on vacation. And set up alerts for properties that hit the market in certain cities because once you buy one property, you will likely want to quickly buy another. This means you need a steady stream of leads to pursue.

Key Takeaways

- Real estate agents will often have the most recent data and listings on available properties.

- Tax auctions can allow you to buy properties for below market value, but can also take more time to close; sometimes more than a year to take possession.

- Talk about properties in terms of "doors," or how many rent checks you are collecting.

- Rising interest rates should not deter you from investing. There will always be a need for long-term rentals, as long as you've bought in an area that is experiencing population growth (or at least isn't shrinking population-wise).

CHAPTER 6

FINANCES AND TAXES

A lthough real estate investing is all about buying properties, to be successful means being profitable. And you can't be profitable unless you know your financials inside and out. After all, the numbers will tell you everything you need to know about your investments. But before you make any money moves, you'll definitely want to speak with your accountant and attorney.

And, even before that, before you start making offers on properties, it's important to set up good financial habits. Now, I realize that if you're looking to invest in real estate, there is an excellent chance that you have already established good financial habits. To be sure we're talking about the same habits, however, let's review the financial habits I think you need in order to be successful. These aren't complicated, but they can be challenging.

Maximize Your Savings

This may seem obvious, but in order to build up a down payment for an investment purchase, or to afford any repairs or upgrades in your properties, or even to ride out months where your tenants don't pay, you need to have savings set aside. To build that up, you should have a budget you're using to guide all of your purchases. With a budget, you can monitor how much you're spending, on what, and how your expenses are trending (up or down).

As part of your budget, you should be setting aside a portion of the funds you earn into a savings account. If you can set up a direct deposit to immediately take a portion of your paycheck and funnel it into a separate savings account, you'll get used to living without that chunk of change.

Ideally, you'll get to a point where you have between three and six months of expenses set aside to cover household expenses if you suddenly lose your job or have a big unanticipated expense. But keep building beyond that six-month cushion so that you have funds readily available to invest when you find a property you like.

While budgeting is short-term focused, to help you better manage the money you have coming in and going out, real estate investing is generally a long-term play for your financial freedom. Unless you're flipping properties shortly after buying them, residential real estate investing typically involves holding a property for at least a year, if not longer. Real estate is an investment vehicle that is fairly stable and appreciates over months and years, not hours and days like more volatile investment tools, like Crypto or stocks, for example.

Creating a Buffer for Expenses

You'll want to continue to set money aside in a savings account even after you buy a property because things always break or go wrong, and you need to have access to money to fix them right away. For example, let's say you've been saving for a while and you have $100,000 in your account. That doesn't mean you should use that whole amount as a down payment on a property. You should really only put down a percentage of what you have saved because unexpected crises are inevitably going to come up, and you want to be prepared. So, if you have $100,000, you might aim to put down $70,000 to $75,000, to leave yourself a $25,000 to $30,000 cushion.

Cushions, or extra funds, are stress-reducers because if something goes wrong, you are able to pay for it. My wife and I had one property with a yard that was swampy, and we couldn't figure out why it was so waterlogged. To fix it required digging up the lawn and putting in a French drain, at a cost of $8,000. If we had put all of our savings down on the house, we wouldn't have been prepared to fix the yard right away. This would have caused us to let the house sit vacant, not generating cash. The solution is to plan ahead, and hold on to funds for these types of situations.

We always put 25% down on a house to buy it and keep money in reserve for the work that will need to be done to get it ready to rent. More recently, my wife and I just closed on a house in Gatlinburg and on our way out of town, we realized that we hadn't set up the cable. That was something we needed to do for our future tenants. Fortunately, we had money set aside for those kinds of expenses. But my point is really that if we had put 100% of our savings down to buy the house, we couldn't have also had the cable (which tenants were expecting) set up and in working order before they arrived.

Usually, you'll need to do more than simply set up cable service, however. At the first cabin we bought, we spent $20,000 after closing to replace flooring, buy new furniture, bedding, light fixtures, and other incidentals. So, on top of the $20,000 it was costing us to renovate the cabin, we also had to factor in the lost rent we weren't receiving for a couple of months while contractors were working. We needed money to make the mortgage payment twice before we started receiving rental income.

If you follow our lead and put 25% down to buy a property and you have $100,000 available, you don't want to buy a $400,000 property, because you'd have nothing left to spend on improvements. If I had $100,000, I'd set aside $25,000 to $30,000 for renovations, which means I'd have $70,000 to put down. With $70,000 as a 25% down payment, that means the properties I should be looking at should cost no more than $280,000, or $250,000 to be even safer.

Since your purchase price is your profitability gauge, if you pay $250,000, you should be confident you can make at least $2,500/ month from it, which is 1%. The one percent rule is a useful rule of thumb when you're looking at rental properties; you want to be able to rent your property for at least 1% of the purchase price per month.

The Profit First Concept

Mike Michalowicz is the author of the business finance book *Profit First*. He advocates taking profit out of the business, or investment in our case, first, followed by your expenses. Together, those two numbers tell you what you need to make each month. This approach is the opposite of how most people handle their finances, which is to pay all of their bills and then bank what's left over. Mike recommends, instead, taking the excess off the top and then covering expenses, to ensure that you're doing your best to keep expenses low.

Capital Gains and Your Finances

When you buy real estate that increases in value, this creates profits. The classification of those profits is either ordinary income for investments held under a year, or capital gains for investments held for more than a year that are profitable. There are only long-term capital gains for investments held for more than a year, not ordinary income (short-term capital gains is a misnomer). And there are different taxes associated with each that you'll want to be aware of.

Holding an asset for less than a year before selling it for a profit is sometimes referred to as short-term capital gains by those who are not being completely accurate. If you sell an asset before reaching 366 days of ownership, you will be taxed at ordinary income tax rates on any profits. Ordinary tax rates are higher than capital gains tax rates, currently set at 22%.

Of course, there could be reasons that you might want to sell a house quickly, such as if you are fixing and flipping it, or if the market suddenly skyrockets in your area. Otherwise, ordinary tax treatment is typically not ideal.

On the other hand, holding an asset beyond the 365th day results in long-term capital gain treatment of the profit made on the sale of that asset, which, as of early 2022 is 22%. Most investors are seeking long-term capital gain treatment because it is generally at a lower tax rate than their own personal rate.

Passive versus Active Income

You've probably heard people talk about wanting a passive income stream, which suggests that they don't have to do much to earn a little money. Although that's a great goal in theory, in real estate investing, the difference is important, as it affects your tax rate. Being an active investor may be a better choice.

Passive Income

In real estate investing, rental net income, limited partnerships, and other types of businesses where the income recipient is not *materially participating* is considered passive income. Because the income is passive, it is usually taxable but treated differently by the IRS. You'll want to become familiar with this concept.

Material Participation

The IRS says that if you have dedicated 500 hours to a business or activity from which you are profiting, that is considered material participation. Also, if you are the only investor and your participation in that business or activity represents all the participation for that year, it is considered material participation. Or, if you have participated up to 100 hours and that is at least as much as anyone else involved in the business, it is considered material participation. It's like the difference between being an amateur and a professional and, as a professional, you can deduct expenses that amateurs cannot.

If you have invested in a property, or in a real estate business, and are not involved in its management at all, the profits you receive would be considered passive income. For example, if you invested $25,000 in a business and the owners paid you a portion of the profits each year, that would be considered passive income. IRS Publication 925 sets out the specific criteria for passive income treatment if you have more questions about what qualifies.

That passive income you receive is taxed anywhere from 10% to 37% currently. The good news is that you can still take passive income deductions to reduce your tax burden. These passive deductions include:

- Property management fees
- Maintenance and repairs
- Utilities
- Landscaping
- Professional and legal fees
- Wages paid to a W-2 employee who receives a salary or hourly wage
- Advertising costs
- Tenant screening fees
- Commission, leasing, and referral fees
- Mortgage interest payments
- Property tax
- Insurance premiums
- License and registration fees
- Travel expenses directly related to the rental property
- Home office expense
- Office supplies
- Telephone and internet

- Dues and subscriptions for professional organizations, such as a real estate investor club
- Continuing education expenses, such as attending seminars or enrolling in courses and coaching
- Depreciation expense to reduce taxable income

Passive income deductions are great, but they are not as advantageous to you as deductions from active income. However, passive income means you are not working every day to manage your portfolio. Hopefully, your investments are paying you each month and supplementing your income earned from your day job.

Active Income

If passive income is money earned without exerting much effort, active is the opposite, requiring a commitment of time and energy. Active income generally refers to wages, tips, salaries, commissions, and other income from materially participating in any activity involving, in this case, your real estate business.

Within the real estate industry, there are two key requirements that must be met to qualify as a material participant:

1. More than half of the personal services you, the taxpayer, performed in all trades or businesses during the year were performed in real property trades or businesses in which you materially participated; AND
2. The taxpayer (meaning you) performed more than 750 hours of services during the tax year in real property trades or businesses in which you materially participated. In truth, it's difficult to hit 750 hours a year unless you're really paying attention to and tracking the hours you spend in your real estate business. On average, you need to spend at least

fourteen hours a week to hit 750 hours a year in your business. The good news is that anything you do related to real estate counts—you just have to have a record of it.

Both of these criteria must be met to qualify as a material participant. Moreover, IRS §469(c)(7)(A) and 26 CFR §469-9(g) requires the taxpayer to make an election on their tax returns—something your accountant will do for you.

Investing 750 hours in real estate activities isn't as impossible as it might sound when you take into account all the types of real estate activities that you can count, such as:

- Conducting market research by scouring MLS listings and online listings
- Scrolling through real estate apps to look at comps for your properties
- Talking to agents, investors, and other property owners
- Attending Meetups or networking events
- Participating in real estate conferences
- Reading about real estate through courses, books, or magazines
- Listening to real estate podcasts while you drive to work
- Writing social media posts or articles about real estate
- Spending time at your properties
- Collecting quotes for work to be done
- Reviewing tenant applications

This is really just the tip of the iceberg, but it will be easier to hit the minimum number if you have a notebook or timekeeping app handy so that you may consistently take note of what you've done with respect to real estate each day.

The Risk of Hiring a Property Manager

If you are self-managing your properties, all of that time can be counted toward the 750-hour minimum needed to qualify as an active real estate professional. But if you hire a property manager, you may be prevented from being considered and there has actually been a legal case where using the services of a property manager disqualified an investor from being considered active. Because the investor was paying someone else to manage the properties, the court decided they were more passive than active participants. This, in turn, impacted their tax situation.

Being categorized as an active participant in real estate allows you to be declared a real estate professional. This means you can deduct many more expenses from the real estate income you earn. The list of deductions passive earners have access to is more limited than what active real estate pros can deduct. This is why it's a smart idea to pursue active participant status.

Whether or not you can offset the tax liability for your own income is going to turn on whether you are active or passive. Passive profits and losses fall into a very different bucket than active, and you can't actually realize losses if you're passive until you sell the property. It's only at the time of sale of a property that you can deduct any losses if you're not materially participating as an active real estate professional.

Key Takeaways

- Spend no more than 70-75% of your savings on down payments; hold on to the rest for repairs and renovations.
- When deciding how long you want to hold a property, consider capital gains taxes.
- You'll want to strongly consider becoming an active real estate professional, rather than a passive investor. Active professionals are permitted to take more tax deductions.

CHAPTER 7

Tax Considerations

While you don't want to make all of your investing decisions based on taxes, it's important to understand how taxes can impact the purchase, rental, and sale of your properties.

Depreciation is Gold

Active real estate professionals want as much depreciation as possible because that depreciation offsets their income. However, you can only deduct up to the amount of income you've earned. But, if you're self-employed, you can offset the income you've earned through your business, or shelter it, by taking as many deductions as you are legally allowed to, including depreciating income-producing properties.

The IRS says that you can deduct a portion of your property's costs each year based on its expected life, which then lowers your taxable income. We'll go through how to calculate that in a minute.

First, there are criteria that you must meet before you can depreciate the property. Pursuant to IRS guidelines, these include:

- You must own the property (you are the owner even if you have a mortgage on the property).
- The property has to be used for business or is income-producing; your personal residence does not qualify.

- The property has a useful life of more than one year.
- And, the property has a determinable useful life, meaning it is not going to decay or wear out.

One caveat is that you can't depreciate a property if you bought and sold it in the same year. Also, the land on which the building sits is not depreciable. Your property is depreciable as soon as you place it into service, meaning as soon as you list it for rent. If you buy it already rented, the clock can start for depreciation on Day 1.

So, how do you calculate how much you can deduct each year on a property? Your depreciation number depends on three things: 1) the basis in the property, 2) the recovery period, and 3) the depreciation method used. Property placed into service after 1986 uses the Modified Accelerated Cost Recovery System (MACRS), which is an accounting mechanism that spreads the life of the property over 27.5 years. The useful life of the property is considered to be 27.5 years for the purposes of depreciation, even though the building itself will likely stand much longer than that.

Here's the step-by-step process:

Determine the basis. Your *basis* is the amount you paid for the property, including all of the additional fees associated with the purchase, such as settlement fees, closing costs, transfer taxes, legal fees, title insurance, surveys, and recording fees. Fees you cannot include as part of your basis are: fire insurance, rent for tenancy prior to closing, charges for refinancing, points paid on the mortgage, appraisals, inspections, and credit reports.

Separate the land and building. Since you can't depreciate land, you have to deduct the value of the land from the property. You can use the assessed real estate tax values to help you determine which portion of the property's value is from the land versus the building, or you can use the fair market value at the time of purchase.

Determine the basis in the house. The basis in your structure needs to be calculated from the date of purchase until it is rent ready. To do this, make sure you include any additions or improvements to the property that have a useful life of at least one year before you put the property into service. Also, if you have added utilities, repaired damage to the property, or paid legal fees that are ordinary and necessary to your business, these can all be included in the calculation of the basis.

Let's run through an example to show you how it works in real life. If you've bought a property for $400,000, when you add all of the fees associated with acquiring it, let's say your total is $435,000. To separate the value of the land and the building, you can use the property tax records to see that, as of the last assessment, the land was worth $100,000, and the improvement (meaning the building) was $300,000. Now you know the building is worth $300,000 of the $435,000 you spent. The $300,000 is the depreciable portion of the asset. The remaining $135,000 is capitalized into the basis of the property. You will need to pull out what you did to the property (the other $35,000) to see if it can be depreciated as well. Remember the HVAC unit that I spoke about in an earlier chapter? If I had bought a $10,000 HVAC unit, I could depreciate that. This is why a good bookkeeper and CPA are so vital.

While depreciation is gold, cost segregation studies can give you platinum, or depreciation on steroids.

Cost Segregation Studies

Cost segregation studies are in-depth examinations of your property that then allow you to take the bulk of the depreciation of that property at the front end of its useful life. You effectively front-load the depreciation you're entitled to take, reducing your taxes even more in the early years of owning the property.

Where you divided your property into land and building in order to calculate the appropriate annual depreciation, cost segregation studies take it a step further—they break your property into all of its parts. That includes everything from the lights to the door knobs, the electrical wiring, the windows, the air conditioning unit, and everything else. Every individual part is identified and segregated into its useful life. Each of those categories will then be depreciated based on the useful life of those assets.

Thus, instead of depreciating your property over 27.5 years, or 39 years for commercial properties, you will have parts of the house that have a useful life of 5 years. Some will have 7 years, and others will be 15-year parts that can be depreciated. This provides you with higher deduction amounts for the property's annual depreciation schedule.

Don't worry, you're not going to conduct this study yourself. You'll want a seasoned tax accountant to handle this for you. But while segmentation studies are complex, a simpler way to reduce your taxes is through proper use of business deductions.

Why I'll Never Pay Off My Home

There are many personal finance gurus out there who recommend paying off your mortgage before you retire. They want you to get a second or third job to generate more income so that you can reduce the mortgage amount. I think that's crazy. After all, with a mortgage, you have a tax deduction and, if you don't pay it off, you'll have money you can then invest in more properties. If you pay your house off, you have hundreds of thousands of dollars locked up in an asset you can't access without refinancing or taking an expensive reverse mortgage. It's hard to grow your real estate investing business if you use your savings to pay off properties, rather than buying more. That's why I don't advise paying off any mortgages, at least for financial reasons. If it's important to you for other reasons, then you should certainly consider it.

Section 1031

Another tool for minimizing your taxes is a 1031 exchange, which can be used to defer capital gains when you sell a property. You can use a 1031 exchange when you buy another property that is similar in cost to the one you sold. This tax mechanism is used to defer capital gains and depreciation recapture. A 1031 exchange allows you to use all your profits from the sale of one property to purchase more real estate. However, in deferring those gains, your basis has to be recalculated.

As a quick refresher, remember that your basis is the amount of money you pay for a piece of property, plus any additional costs to acquire the property. For example, if you buy a property for $100,000 and pay $5,000 in closing costs to the bank and an attorney, your basis becomes $105,000.

In a general 1031 exchange, the new property purchased is the cost of that property minus any gain you deferred in the exchange.

This simple concept quickly gets complicated since the real estate basis changes over time and usually increases. That increase in your basis is called adjusted basis. The reasons that your basis adjusts are mainly twofold:

1. By improving the property in some way, such as through a bathroom renovation, renovating a common area, or adding on to a property, these capital expenditures are added to increase your total basis in the property.

2. Similarly, depreciation expenses of that property serve to reduce your basis. Depreciation expense allows an investor to lower his/her income by depreciating the property over a number of years. Depreciation also reduces your basis and can lead to tax liability when you sell the property outside of a 1031 exchange. It does this through depreciation deductions on your tax returns. By taking depreciation as a deduction, you are reducing your basis because you are deducting your basis through depreciation.

Here is how to calculate the cost basis of your new property:

- Figure the adjusted basis for the property you have just sold. This includes any mortgage you took to acquire the property. Your mortgage counts as basis in the property.

- Add the value of any other property you transfer in the exchange (meaning, the new property you're buying), the mortgage amount on your new property, the amount of cash you are contributing to the new purchase, and any recognized gain on the sold property.
- Subtract any money or property you received in the exchange, the amount of the mortgage on the sold property, and any recognized loss on any property sold in the exchange.

These steps result in the basis for your newly acquired property in the 1031 exchange. Take note that the purchase price for the new property does not play a role in determining cost basis. (Surprising to most investors, I know!)

For example, let's say you perform a 1031 exchange by selling a property for $300,000. You have a mortgage of $150,000 on the property at the time of the sale, and your adjusted cost basis in the property is $170,000. You complete the exchange by purchasing a $500,000 property with a mortgage of $250,000.

In this case, you calculate your new basis by taking the original property's adjusted basis ($170,000), adding your new mortgage ($250,000), and subtracting the original property's outstanding mortgage ($150,000). This gives you a new tax basis of $270,000. This new basis has nothing to do with what you actually paid for your new home, however.

Although 1031 exchanges can be very useful, sometimes it is worth taking the capital gain tax treatment if you are buying up. What does that really mean? Let me give you an example:

- You buy a property in year 1 for $250,000.
- You sell the property in year 3 for $450,000.
- During the time that you owned the property, you depreciated the asset, resulting in adjusted basis.
- Through the sale, you will make approximately $200,000 in capital gains ($450,000-$250,000=$200,000).

- In this scenario, you would owe capital gains tax on the $200,000 and would have to recapture that depreciation taken. This means that all the deductions for depreciation that have been taken over the years will have to be brought back into your income.

Fortunately, there is another option if you don't want to pay capital gains on the sale. You could take that $200,000 gain and buy a more expensive property. Let's say it costs $800,000. You could then take advantage of new depreciation to offset the depreciation recapture and offset your capital gains.

In order to determine the correct dollar amounts you need to spend to achieve this tipping point, you will need to work the numbers. But don't get so caught up in deferring capital gains that you miss an opportunity to buy a property that may be a better fit for your plans.

Understanding the impact of property dispositions from a tax standpoint is vital to the management and growth of your portfolio. Rely on your team of advisors to help you navigate any disposition of your real estate so that you achieve the optimal outcome for you and your future.

Key Takeaways

- Maximize the depreciation you take on your properties, to reduce your tax obligations.
- Cost segregation studies are in-depth examinations of your property that then allow you to take the bulk of the depreciation of that property at the front end of its useful life, reducing your taxes even more in the early years of owning the property.
- Consider using a 1031 exchange when you buy another property that is similar in cost to the one you sold, which enables you to defer capital gains and depreciation recapture. You can use all your profits from the sale of one property to purchase more real estate.

CHAPTER 8

HOW TO VALUE A POTENTIAL INVESTMENT

To say that investors want to make a profit on their real estate purchase is a truism. Of course, investors want to make a profit! However, in the real estate world there are several ways to measure profits, from return on investment (ROI), to capitalization rate (Cap Rate), Capital Expenditure (CapEx), cash-on-cash, or the 1-2% rule, among a few other metrics. Those calculations tell you how much value you derived from your property. And the lingo, or the terminology, is important for you to understand so that you pick up on what real estate agents, investors, or property managers are telling you. Knowing the language is key, especially when starting out.

However, your ability to come out ahead on your investment has a lot to do with how little you pay for it up front, much like stocks. In the COVID era, post-2020, that's become harder to do in many markets. Because demand has skyrocketed, real estate sellers have taken the opportunity to increase the asking price for their properties. Much of this, but not all, is being driven by people in high-tax states looking to move into lower tax states. For example, we're seeing residents of California deciding to relocate to Montana, Texas, Florida, Tennessee, and other low-tax or no-tax states.

The Economics of Supply and Demand

High housing prices can become a problem for investors who just want to get into the market, as well as for home buyers planning to stick around for several years. The prices are exorbitant and, in some places, barely affordable! And that causes issues for appraisals because it's likely there aren't comparable properties that have sold for such inflated prices recently.

I was just dealing with this exact scenario a couple of weeks ago on behalf of one of my clients. He and his fiancée moved from California to Tennessee about a year ago and have been looking at homes, trying to decide where they wanted to settle, and finally found what they'd been looking for and put an offer in, which was accepted.

They bought the house for $635,000, which was well within his budget, but the appraisal only came in at $432,000, more than $200,000 lower than the purchase price. I've never seen such a huge discrepancy between an appraised value and the seller's asking price. And that is a problem if you're counting on bank financing, which only loans up to 70% or 80% of the property's value.

The buyer shared the appraisal with the seller, who then agreed to sell him the property at $5,000 over the appraised value. My client agreed to pay $437,000, but the seller decided in the meantime that he wanted to back out because he was advised that he might be able to get more from another buyer. Since we have a signed contract at $437,000, we're now in litigation.

On the other hand, there are also buyers who are buying homes sight unseen because they can get more space for less money outside of major cities like Los Angeles. One woman I know moved to Tennessee from California—because Tennessee doesn't have an income tax it's become quite popular recently—after buying a home online. She found the home on the MLS system, bought it, moved in, and now has decided the home isn't quite up to her standards.

Because the square footage of the home and the size of the yard were probably multiples of what she had in California, she bought it, and only after moving in did she discover that the area has a little more crime than she's comfortable with. Now she's suing the agents and sellers, arguing that they somehow conspired to sell her this property.

You should always check out properties to be sure they are what you're looking for, especially if you don't know the area. This is even more critical if you're buying a personal home for you and your family. As an investor, your perspective is a little different and your primary concern is likely that it can be profitable, rather than whether you like the exterior paint color or yard size.

Know Your Numbers

The difference with rental real estate is that, in addition to being a safe place to invest your money, even if the market corrects and prices plummet, a correction will have less of an impact on your ability to rent your property. People still need a place to live. And while the 1% rule—that the rent you receive should at least be equal to 1% of the property's purchase price—has become harder to achieve thanks to skyrocketing asking prices, it's still possible to make money in rental real estate. Properties that meet the 1% guideline are more likely to be found from an investor looking to sell a few properties off and take some money out. Many are willing to sell for a reasonable profit, but they aren't out to gouge anyone since they probably bought the place for a fraction of what it's worth now anyway.

It can be hard to distinguish which properties will be profitable and which won't, however. This is why I want to share some of the terminology investors use when describing real estate. These are the formulas they use, and that you should use, in order to understand the information that's being shared with you about available properties, because a property can look very different, depending on how you intend to use it.

Right now, short-term rentals are beating long-term rentals in terms of profits, by a long shot. Where there is stability and less work with a long-term renter, there are higher profits available with a short-term rental through Airbnb or Vrbo, for example.

This fact was driven home for me when I was talking to a client about a property in the South that looks like an eleven-unit motel but is set up as an Airbnb. The asking price on it was much higher than I expected, and out of line with the comparables in the area by about $2 million. Yes, it was grandfathered in to the short-term rental zoning so it could be used as a legitimate Airbnb rental but because it had no rental history, there is no way of knowing if it could be profitable.

Those are just some of the questions a lender or a syndicate will ask before they're willing to put their money in. Some of the facts and figures they'll want to get from you include the projected ROI, CapEx, Cap Rate, and Modification Rule, on top of the 1-2% rule. So, what are those different measurements and how do you use them?

Return on Investment (ROI)

Return on investment, or ROI, is probably the most commonly used term in investing. It's also the first metric you want to look at when evaluating different potential investments. In simple terms, ROI measures the percentage of return on a property over a certain period of time, or, for every $1 you invest in a property, how much will you earn back.

One way to calculate ROI on a longer-term investment is to take the present value minus the cost of the property, divided by the cost of the property, times 100. That's your ROI in percentage terms. For example, if you bought a property for $250,000 and with an investment of $25,000 increased its value to $350,000, the calculation looks like this:

ROI = (($350,000-($250,000+25,000) ÷ ($250,000+$25,000) x 100 = 27.27%

That means you'll get a 27% return on your investment if the numbers hold true. That's a good deal.

Conversely, if you bought a property for $500,000, invested nothing, and five years later it's worth $550,000, your return on investment is 10%.

You can also use ROI to look at income generated from rental properties. Using a slightly different version of the formula, you can take the annual cash generated by the property after accounting for operating expenses and your mortgage payment, divided by the total of what you invested.

The equation looks like this:

ROI = Annual Return ÷ Total Investment

Here is an example: Property of $100,000 that generates $10,000 before debt service

Down payment of 25% ($25,000), your total investment would be $25,000

The loan is $75,000 over 15 years at 3.75% for a monthly payment of $545.42 (Principal and Interest (P&I))

The equation then becomes: ($10,000-($545.42 x 12))÷$25,000 = $3,454.96÷$25,000 = .13819 or 13.819%

The rental property with the higher ROI is typically the best investment. By using different down payment amounts, you can see how the ROI changes to help you decide how best to leverage your investment. Investors focused on maximizing ROI will want to use as little money down as possible, despite the annual return being lower. That said, I typically advise investors to put some skin in the game by staking out good equity in the event your market is seeing appreciation rise year over year. Higher down payments also generally receive more favorable rates from banks.

CapEx

CapEx is an abbreviation for capital expenditures, which are funds used to acquire, upgrade, and maintain physical assets, such as property, plant, equipment, or technology. It's what an investor or buyer would spend to purchase and update the property.

CapEx on fixed assets includes repairing roofs, buying equipment, replacing air conditioning units, or adding a retaining wall, for example. CapEx does not include routine maintenance, like repairing a plumbing leak. Expenditures that are considered capital-related are what is required for the property to function properly.

For example, a couple of years ago we had a tree fall on the roof of a property we own in Chattanooga. Obviously, the roof needed to be repaired, but when we toured the house, we saw that the foundation had been damaged as well. When you walked from the front of the house to the back, there was an obvious sloping of the floor by about twelve inches. It had to be corrected, and because all of that work was being done to bring the house back to full functionality, the cost was considered a CapEx. We weren't adding value to the property, unfortunately. We were only bringing the house back to be totally habitable.

If this had happened while the house was for sale, those expenses would need to be capitalized into the purchase price, meaning added on to the cost of the property. It becomes part of your basis, though it can't become part of your mortgage. So, if the property was worth, say, $200,000 and the cost of repairs due to the tree falling was $50,000, your new basis is $250,000—$200,000 from the purchase and $50,000 for the repairs, which you'd need to pay out of pocket.

One way to determine what kind of capital expenditures might be required, both in the short- and long-term, is to ask for and review the maintenance reports. They can give you a sense of what may need to be done soon, what maintenance and repairs have been deferred, and what is a recent addition or renovation.

In some instances, you can use that information as part of your purchase price negotiation if you're trying to buy the property. But some sellers are unwilling to come down in price, especially during a seller's market.

The formula for calculating CapEx is:

CapEx = Change in property, plant, and equipment + current depreciation

Your current depreciation is calculated based on the useful life of the property. A commercial property's depreciation schedule is 39 years and a residential property is 27.

Cash-on-Cash

Another metric you'll hear used is cash-on-cash, which is basically a calculation used to estimate the return from the asset generating the income, meaning your property. It refers to the total amount of distributions paid annually (also known as income) as a percentage of its current price.

Cash-on-cash = annual net cash flow/invested equity

For example, if the property you're looking at is priced at $400,000 and it generates a monthly income of $2,000, the cash-on-cash yield on an annual basis would be 6%. That's because the annual cash flow is $2,000 x 12, which equals $24,000. When you divide that by $400,000, you get 6%.

That's not a bad return. Ideally, you'd get much more than 6%, but I wouldn't go below 6%. At 5% or lower, it's just not worth doing the deal because you're not making enough money.

Separating Profit Centers

Airbnb and the new short-term rental market have completely changed how people are evaluating deals. If a property has multiple areas that can be rented, you can create separate profit centers. For example, you could rent the main house out at one nightly or weekly rate and the unit over the garage at another. Or, if there is a basement unit you could create, that could be another separate rental unit. Each additional rental unit means more potential cash flow coming in each month, which can help pay down your mortgage or provide funds for an investment in another property.

Cap Rate

Cap rate has multiple definitions, but the one I'm talking about concerns the present value of your future benefits. So, where CapEx is about your expenditures, or what you're going to spend to make your property more valuable, the cap rate is the anticipated return on that expenditure.

Getting more detailed, the cap rate is a formula that divides the net operating income (NOI) generated by the property before the debt service (principal and interest), by the property value or its asking price. The formula looks like this:

Cap Rate = NOI÷Property Value

Debt for the mortgage payment should be excluded from the cap rate calculation because investors leverage property differently. For example, let's say you are looking at a property with an annual gross income of $24,000 per year. If your normal operating expenses are 50% of your annual gross income, the NOI will be $12,000 per year ($24,000 x .50).

If the property has an asking price of $240,000, the projected cap rate will be 5%. ($12,000÷$240,000 = .05 or 5%)

Cap rates are going to be different depending on the market you are looking at. For example, Nashville is going to be different from Stowe, Vermont. Generally, the higher the cap rate, the better the investment, since the potential return is going to be higher, all things being equal. That said, if there is a property with a cap rate outside the norm for the market, take some extra time and dig into why that is. What is it that sets that property apart? While not always a problem property, it does merit some more investigation. You may have found a diamond in the rough or you may have found a dumpster fire. You'll want to find out which it is before you make an offer.

It is wise to continually evaluate your cap rate. If property values drop, if rents get depressed, etc., then you need to evaluate what is affecting your cap rate and your investment. If your cap rate is dropping, it may be because your CapEx is increasing, or other costs are increasing. That means your once-performing asset may not be performing at all anymore.

When evaluating properties, you want to look for properties with a higher cap rate because that indicates that the value of the property is increasing.

The 1-2% Rule

My personal favorite evaluation of real estate investment is called the 1-2% rule, which you've heard me use before. This is a guideline, or what you should aim to meet or exceed when buying a property for rental.

The rule suggests that after all expenses are paid, you should net at least 1% or 2% of the purchase price of the property each month. This means that if you buy a $100,000 property, you want to net $1,000 a month after you have paid all expenses. However, with real estate so hot right now, I have moved to a modified 1% rule, since it's now much more difficult to net 1% or 2% of the purchase price.

What I mean is that because it can be very difficult to net even 1% of the purchase price in many markets today, you'll want to aim for 1% or 2%, but recognize that if you can at least cover all of your expenses, including mortgage payment, taxes, and other maintenance and repair costs, that may be enough to warrant proceeding with the purchase of a property. With that income, your tenant is covering all of your costs while your property appreciates.

Regardless of the formula you use to evaluate a property's potential, you're going to hear these formulas frequently from other investors and your team of advisors. These are good terms to know, so you can speak with authority with possible buyers and sellers.

Key Takeaways

- There are several ways to measure profits, from return on investment (ROI), to capitalization rate (cap rate), CapEx, cash-on-cash, or the 1-2% rule, among others.

- Before you buy property, a good idea is to visit the area, to see the area and to spot potential negatives that weren't in any of the photos the agent took.

- A good rule of thumb is that the rent you receive should be equal to 1% of the house's purchase price.

- ROI is probably the most commonly used term in investing. It measures the percentage of return on a property over a certain period of time, or, for every $1 you invest in a property, how much you will earn back.

- When evaluating properties, you want to look for properties with a higher cap rate, because that indicates that the value of the property is increasing.

- Where CapEx is about your expenditures, or what you're going to spend to make your property more valuable, the cap rate is the anticipated return on that expenditure.

CHAPTER 9

───∿───

UNDERSTANDING YOUR FINANCING OPTIONS

Many new real estate investors leverage their personal assets in order to buy their first property. This makes a lot of sense for a couple of reasons. The first is that your personal residence, if you own it, is likely one of your larger assets and you can typically borrow against your equity in it to buy another property. A second reason is that applying for financing as an individual, rather than as a company, is less expensive. You can qualify for individual mortgage rates rather than commercial, which is higher. You can own up to ten properties as an individual, so you won't limit your expansion potential by starting out this way.

At some point, however, you may opt to start buying properties as business assets. That will impact your financing options. But the easiest way to start real estate investing is to rely on your personal assets and credit to finance your first property. Here's how many investors get started:

Personal Loans

A friend of mine is currently investigating ways to get into real estate investing. We were talking the other day about what he can do to move the needle on his personal wealth. I had already told him he needed to buy a rental property, so after this most recent conversation, he took some action.

Your typical sources of a down payment for an investment property are:

- Personal savings
- HELOC against a primary residence
- Retirement savings

My friend got a home equity line of credit (HELOC) from his bank against his personal residence. That HELOC is going to be his down payment on a new property because he doesn't want to dip into his personal savings. So, he's leveraging his home so that he can buy a multifamily property, either a duplex or quadplex, which he'll place in a newly formed LLC.

He could use his savings for that down payment, which many people do. You always have to have something to put down, whether it's from savings or investments or a HELOC. In this case, he has opted not to use cash, but to leverage the equity in his private residence. And when his new property starts generating rent payments, he can use those profits to pay the HELOC off, on top of paying his mortgage note.

Using a Self-Directed IRA to Invest in Real Estate

More people are starting to use self-directed IRAs to invest in real estate. Self-directed IRAs are a great way to leverage what you've already saved to invest for your retirement, but this strategy is really more appropriate for someone who wants to get into real estate investing more seriously than just owning a vacation home that they rent from time to time. Once established, you can use the funds in your IRA to invest in properties. There are companies that specialize in setting up self-directed IRAs.

Banks want to see a minimum down payment of 20% to 25% of the purchase price, which you should use as a guide to determine what price points you should be looking at. If you have $100,000, and you recall our discussion in the previous chapter about holding back a good portion of those funds for renovations and as a resource if tenants stop paying rent, you know that as a general rule you don't want to put down any more than, say, $70,000. This means that, with that amount, you should be looking at properties that cost no more than $280,000 to $350,000, depending on your down payment percentage. But that should be your maximum. Don't overextend yourself to the point that you're uncomfortable.

A better approach would be to explore smaller markets where finding lower-priced properties is easier. For example, if you only have $10,000 to put down, you need to go into a smaller market where you can get a $40,000 or $50,000 home. They do still exist, believe it or not.

Ultra-Cheap Old Houses

One resource to find super low-priced houses that are often in need of some serious rehab is the subscription electronic newsletter Ultra-Cheap Old Houses. There is a small monthly fee, currently at $6, which earns you weekly listings of US homes priced at under $25,000—"serious fixer-uppers," they call them. You can learn more at www.cheapold-houses.com.

So, you can borrow money from your HELOC for a down payment, you can tap into your savings for a down payment, or you can do what I did and liquidate your retirement savings. I wouldn't generally recommend using your retirement savings because if you're younger than 59 ½, you'll pay penalties and interest for tapping into that money early. But I took a gamble that my investment would more than cover the penalties I would be assessed for doing that. So far, it was a good move.

One property we bought a couple of years ago with some of that money was a property in Chattanooga that cost $183,000. It appraised at $170,000, however, so we had to come to closing with the $13,000 difference between the purchase price and the bank's appraisal price, on top of our 25% down payment.

Less than two years later, we're about to sell it for $255,000. It was rented when we bought it, we didn't make any improvements, and now we're selling it for a $70,000 profit after just sitting on it for a couple of years.

Seller Financing

Another potential financing option is seller financing if the owner of the property you're interested in is willing to hold the promissory note. Typically, with seller financing, you put anywhere from 5% to 15% down, and then the seller holds the mortgage. You pay the seller the monthly payment, just as you would a bank.

Now, you may wonder why a seller would do this. One reason is that they've owned the property forever, so they own it outright—which is a requirement—but instead of taking a lump sum by selling it through a real estate agent, the seller can enjoy monthly income by financing the sale themselves.

Another reason is that the seller may have become tired of being a landlord. If they've been renting the property for a few years, they may be ready to hand over the reins to a new owner and step back from the maintenance and repair duties.

Or, maybe the market has declined and getting financing has become more challenging. If buyers can't get loans, the seller can't recoup his or her investment, so they may opt to finance the sale themselves to make the sale possible. Seller financing is more common than you might think.

How Many Properties Can You Personally Finance?

Fannie Mae, the government agency involved in home mortgages, recently increased the number of properties individual investors can purchase using conventional financing from four to ten. That means that an individual can finance up to ten properties using consumer mortgages, rather than commercial loans. You can still hold those properties in an LLC, but until you're ready to buy your eleventh property, you can continue to finance them using conventional 15-year or 30-year mortgages.

Hard Money Lenders

Although I was willing to take a risk and withdraw funds from my retirement account, which, really, no one recommends, I want to caution you against using hard money lenders without really thinking it through. Hard money means you're going to pay a much higher interest rate for the use of the money—it's expensive.

People offering hard money loans are typically using their self-directed IRAs to make high-interest loans, and they also expect a piece of the profit on top of that. That can work if you're looking at a BRRRR (or buy, rehab, rent, refinance, repeat process) where you expect to be able to get your money out fairly soon. But it doesn't make as much sense to use hard money on a long-term rental investment. If you're holding onto a property long-term, you're going to be paying high interest long-term, which makes it difficult for the property to be profitable.

Partnerships

If you need money and don't want to turn to hard money lenders, you can also consider bringing in a partner who is your money person. This arrangement can work if they supply the cash to buy and renovate the properties you locate and negotiate to buy, but then you need to become the property manager and be responsible for any maintenance and repairs. In those situations, they're more like a silent partner and you're providing the sweat equity.

Partnerships can work as long as you both are clear about expectations. What, exactly, is each person responsible for in this venture? These arrangements tend to fall apart when one partner feels that the other isn't pulling their weight, so just clarify everything up front to avoid that.

When you reach your ten-property maximum, it's time to look into commercial loans.

How Commercial Loans Work

Commercial loans have shorter terms than residential loans, which are usually either 15- or 30-year notes. My wife and I typically get 5-year notes, but they're amortized over 20 years. That means that at the 5-year mark, we refinance the mortgage. So the mortgage is a 5-year term, but the monthly payments are based on a 20-year payoff, or 240 payments (12 x 20) rather than 60 (12 x 5). The result is that the monthly payments are smaller.

Commercial Financing

Although commercial mortgages are a little more expensive, due to interest rates tending to be slightly higher and shorter term, commercial banks can be far more creative. I've found that they will work hard to make a deal work for you. However, the actual approval and closing processes are almost exactly the same as with conventional mortgages.

The Mortgage Qualification Process

Whether you're pursuing conventional financing for your property or a commercial loan, the qualification process is almost exactly the same. The bank, or your lender, wants to understand your financial situation so it can assess the risk of you not being able to pay your mortgage on time each month. The bank wants to see how much money you have coming in, and how much you are obligated to spend to pay your existing debt obligations. You'll be asked to supply, among other things:

- Checking account statements
- Investment account statements
- Retirement account statements
- A mortgage statement on any properties you currently own
- Tax returns for the last three years, for personal and business
- A list of your collateral
- All outstanding debt, including credit cards, loans, mortgages, and car notes
- Pay stub to prove your monthly income

On top of your background financial statements, the lender will also run a credit report to see if there are any debts you haven't listed and which would affect your repayment abilities.

After the bank has the chance to check all of your information over and run some numbers, they will let you know if you have pre-approval to proceed with a mortgage and the maximum amount the bank will lend you.

My wife and I started out with traditional 30-year notes using conventional financing. When we moved over to commercial lending, we switched to 5-year/15-year amortization and 5-year/20-year amortization deals. Some banks are even willing to do 5-year notes with 25-year amortization, which lowers the monthly payment even further while you cash flow the property.

Although you're borrowing as a business, banks still require a personal guarantee from you at the outset. However, some banks will drop the personal guarantee on the property once you get to 50% loan-to-value on the property. Let me give you an example of what a 50% loan-to-value might look like. Let's say you own a property worth $1 million and owe $500,000 on it. The loan-to-value is exactly 50% in that instance. But when the bank looks at the property's appreciation and the cash flow it is generating, the amount you owe will drop below 50%, which will often eliminate the need for your personal guarantee.

Dropping the personal guarantee is a great thing for you personally, but at the end of the day, you need to decide if you want to owe less on a property or use that equity to buy more properties. That is a business decision, and a very important one for you to make at some point.

You could do a cash out refinance and pull money out to invest in another property. For example, let's say you buy a $3 million property and hold it for ten years. Now, when the property is worth $7 million, you can do a cash out refinance (also known as a "refi") to extract some of the equity you've built up thanks to the appreciation through the years. What you're doing with that refi is basically taking the equity out, which is not considered income to you because it's a loan, and then using it to buy another property or two. It's a way of leveraging up. And the great thing is that the equity you've effectively pulled out and which is considered as debt is not considered income, so it's not taxable.

Please read that last paragraph again and think about what it could mean for you. By buying a property, letting it appreciate, then refinancing it and buying another, repeating the process over and over, you're building a valuable real estate portfolio without ever paying taxes on the equity you extracted from each additional purchase. This is huge!

The underwriting process for commercial loans is also more scrupulous, as they look more carefully at the property rent history—they'll want to see that, incidentally. If you're purchasing a property that has not previously been rented, but you intend to rent it, you'll want to prepare some written materials to spell out how the property has been used and how it will be used going forward, with projections for the rent to be earned in the future.

We had to do exactly that after buying a cabin that had a poor rental history. Fortunately, there was a reason that could easily be explained to the bank: the owners used it for themselves, primarily, and only rented it occasionally. The little bit of income they did earn each year wasn't much—I think it ended up being around $17,000. So, we had to prepare financial projections to show that we anticipated making at least $50,000/year from the property once it was put on a rental program managed by a professional property management firm.

If you're considering buying a property that hasn't been previously rented, you can and should call a local property rental office and ask what the average rent is for a typical property in the area, with similar features and amenities. You can explain that you intend to rent the property you're interested in buying and wondered what they see as a reasonable rent rate, based on the current market. The rental office should be able to pull up information on the area that the property is in and tell you, while you're on the phone, what similar properties rent for, and how easy it is to rent them.

You can then turn that information you've gathered into a typewritten report on the rental potential of the property for the lender to consider. You can also tell the bank to feel free to call the person you spoke with at the property rental firm to confirm the numbers.

Although I wouldn't start with a commercial note, it is certainly doable once you have a few properties under your belt.

Personally, if I were starting over, I'd first go with the conventional 30-year note. Your mortgage rate will be low, so your monthly payments will be low, which gives you greater opportunity to make a good profit. The first type of property I would look at would be a single-family home, maybe a three-bedroom, two-bath home that you could rent out to a family. Nothing fancy, and in the early stages, you want to get your feet wet with something that isn't high risk. Start small. Don't swing for the fences by getting into distressed real estate or anything if you don't have experience in that area.

Money at Closing

Although you often hear about people bringing money to closings, where you take ownership and possession of the property you just bought, that's seldom the case anymore. Today, your bank typically wires your down payment funds. The only time you would bring a check is if you were making up a gap somewhere, such as if the appraisal came in too low.

At closing, you're really just there to sign papers. All the money that is changing hands is worked out in advance, with your bank instructed to wire your down payment to the title company. The bank service fees, attorney's fees, title fees, and other expenses are typically rolled into the mortgage.

The average closing cost is a percentage of the property value. Typically, attorney's fees are around $500 to $600. You'll also pay the prorated portion of the taxes and insurance, and there is a bank fee. All of these fees will be spelled out on your closing document, which you'll receive in advance of the actual closing. Your attorney, agent, or title company should send that statement for you to review in advance. You should never be surprised by anything that comes up at the actual closing because you should have been notified in advance of everything that will happen and what you'll actually be paying.

After your hand gets a cramp from signing so many documents, you're done. Either you or your real estate agent will be given the keys to the property. Depending on whether you'll be doing any work on it or not, you may want to immediately turn the keys over to your property manager so they can get in there and have a look around.

Rarely do I have things go sideways by the time we get to closing because, at that point, the deal has effectively been done. The money has been transferred and all that's left is to sign a ream of papers. But I recently had a situation where we were supposed to close on a property on Monday, but on Friday afternoon, I received a call from the property manager informing us that if the sellers didn't receive a check on the day of closing (which is Monday), the deal is off.

This sounded ludicrous to me since I had made the down payment, was approved for the loan, had coordinated the closing-by-mail with the sellers' title company, and had authorized the bank to transfer funds. Although I don't control how quickly their bank moves the funds into their account, apparently the sellers were adamant that they *had* to receive the money on the day of closing.

I called the attorney at the title company because that was who had told the sellers that they should receive their money on the day of closing. That attorney was somehow under the mistaken belief that, unless the sellers received their money right after the closing, the closing was in some way invalid, or that ownership really hadn't changed hands. I was baffled. He seemed unaware of how things worked.

So, I educated him, letting him know that if the sellers interfered with the closing on Monday, I would slap a lien *lis pendens* on the property that would make it difficult to sell for years. A lien *lis pendens* is a lien that is placed on a property after a lawsuit has been filed by someone who has a property interest, which I did since it was under contract. They backed off, we closed as expected, but that was a situation where the sellers had not been sufficiently briefed about how the closing process worked.

Communication is key throughout the real estate purchase process to avoid any surprises or mishaps that can end up costing you money. Make sure both buyer and seller understand the process fully and that their expectations have been set appropriately so that everything runs smoothly. You don't want your money tied up because of a misstep or miscommunication.

Even before that, however, make sure the financing product you're using is the right one for you and your situation. There are many products available to you, so go with the product and the lender that will best meet your needs.

Key Takeaways

- Your two basic options when it comes to real estate finance are a conventional mortgage, based on your personal finances and assets, or a commercial loan tied to your business.

- You can have up to ten conventional mortgages in your name before you have to use commercial lenders.

- Other financing options for individual borrowers include tapping into personal savings, setting up a home equity line of credit (HELOC) against a personal residence, withdrawing from retirement savings, or using a self-directed IRA, hard money lender, or forming a partnership.

- Real estate closings today are all about signing paperwork. Rarely do you need to bring a check for anything at the closing; money changing hands is generally arranged in advance unless you have to make up the difference between an appraisal and purchase price.

CHAPTER 10

———w———

FINDING MONEY TO BUY PROPERTIES

You've heard that "it takes money to make money," which is certainly true. But that money doesn't necessarily have to come from your personal bank account. And there is no magic number that you need to have set aside for real estate investing before you get started.

You can actually have no money to start. While I don't recommend it, there are definitely ways to get into deals with no money of your own. You'll still need to invest your time and talent, but in some cases, you can partner with someone on a property and own a percentage in exchange for your sweat equity.

Find a Partner

The simplest way to obtain an ownership stake in a property without any money of your own is to find a money person—that is, someone who has money to invest, but who may not have the time to take care of all the other tasks associated with finding, buying, and managing an investment property. That's where you can contribute.

Let me give you a scenario to explain how such an arrangement could work. Let's say we have a guy named John Jones. John is in his fifties and has money just lying around, available to be invested. He sees what's going on in the economy and he wants to diversify his investments with real estate.

He has a couple of options. One is to use his money to buy into a real estate syndicate, where several people pool their money and together buy a large property. Or, he can buy a piece of property and manage it himself. But he has no interest in doing that and, really, no time, since he works full-time. The other option is to find someone to whom he can offer a percentage of equity in the deal in exchange for managing the property. In that case, not only does he save on property management fees, but he gains a partner who has a vested interest in taking care of that building (probably better than an outside property manager would, too).

This happens more often than you might expect.

What are syndication deals?

You may have heard of real estate syndicates. Essentially, they are a group of people who want to buy a large property, such as, say, an apartment complex. Let's say the purchase price is $20 million, and few individuals have that kind of cash. So, they pull together a group of people, some of whom will be general partners (who are also called sponsors) and others who will be limited partners.

Banks need to see that you have a sufficient down payment to buy a property. On a $20 million property, you need 20% to buy it, or $4 million. The general partners often put some money in and are responsible for underwriting it and managing it. The limited partners are the money, and they receive a preferred return in exchange for putting up the funds to make the deal happen.

The last syndication deal I did was worth $23 million. The five general partners each put in $100,000 and then gathered a group of accredited investors (who qualify as sophisticated by IRS rules), who, as limited partners, each invested anywhere between $25,000 and $500,000.

The person who doesn't bring money to the table can take care of tasks the money person doesn't have the interest or time to do, such as:

- Drive neighborhoods in search of potential properties to purchase
- Regularly combing MLS listings to see what's available or new to the market
- Sending out mailers to property owners in certain areas
- Underwriting a property to make sure all the numbers work and that the property has profit potential
- Renovating a property to get it ready to rent or sell
- Cleaning a property in between renters
- Managing a property to keep it in the best possible condition and ensure that tenants or renters are happy

This scenario can be ideal for a person who has time on their hands, but not a huge bank account.

So, how do you find these types of deals? There are a number of places where you can connect with people who may need your time and skills, such as:

- BiggerPockets Meetups
- Local real estate investing group meetings
- Facebook groups for real estate investors
- Local real estate agents and property managers

These are just some starting points, however. You need to create your own network of people who can refer you to investors who need property managers or maintenance people, or who need someone to check out a neighborhood or property. That can be formed through your existing friends and acquaintance network.

For example, I do Brazilian Jiu Jitsu (BJJ) four or five times a week and inevitably, while I'm training, another student will start asking me questions about how to get into real estate investing. It's a natural conversation that starts with them asking what you do, or vice versa, and you telling them that you're getting into real estate investing.

One time, a younger guy asked me, "How can I do this without any money?"

So, I asked, "Okay, if you don't have money, what value can you bring? Can you go find properties? Can you cut the grass? Can you fix a broken door? Can you replace a window? Because if you can, that's worth money to me because it means I can hire you and not a property manager. If you can do that, I'll give you 5% of the deal." And that's how it starts.

It's not a get-rich-quick scheme, but you can definitely get rich slowly this way.

Why Mobile Home Parks Can be Lucrative

Although there are fewer areas today where you can find a property for under $100,000, one type of investing is in mobile home parks. With the housing market having a significant shortage of inventory (a.k.a. scarcity), many people are looking at mobile or manufactured housing as an economical alternative to traditional housing.

Mobile home parks are tremendously lucrative. They're also a little unconventional because the tenant rents the pad (which is the concrete slab that the manufactured home or trailer sits on) from you, and pays all the utilities. The tenant will never own the land that the home sits on in that situation, but you can also buy a mobile home and rent it out and do quite well. Owning the land (pad) and the trailer is a very attractive situation.

As long as your renter is paying more than enough to cover your note on the land and other infrastructure costs, the rent on the pad plus rent on the home should be cash flow positive. Offering a rent-to-own on a mobile home is also a good idea because someone who intends to one day own the property will generally take better care of it than someone who plans to move out after a year or two.

Keep in mind, however, that mobile homes don't appreciate; they depreciate. They're not terribly valuable, which is why you can generally buy them for $20,000 or $30,000, at least at the moment. But if your buyer ends up not completing the deal, you can at least sell it back to the manufacturer. The manufacturer will refurbish it and you can buy a replacement unit. I see a lot of potential here.

Why lease-to-own is a smart idea

Whether you're renting a mobile home or single-family home, if you're interested in selling it in the near future, a rent-to-own deal could work out well for you. Instead of renting your place for a set amount each month for a year at a time, you could agree to sell it for a certain amount, with the renter paying a monthly rate that, over time, will pay off the note that you hold. You need a contract in place to specify how it will work, and what happens if they get behind or move.

Essentially, if they fail to pay on time, they lose all the money they have built up as a credit that goes toward the purchase of the unit. This is generally an incentive to pay in a timely fashion and, because it's theirs, they'll take good care of it, which is great if you end up having to re-rent it down the line.

Another option, beyond mobile homes, is tiny homes, which are quite popular right now. (There are even HGTV shows about tiny homes, including "Tiny House, Big Living," and "Tiny House Hunters.") If you buy land, you can put tiny homes on them and rent them out on a nightly basis through Airbnb. There are plenty of people who are curious about them, so if you have a good location, such as in a popular vacation destination, you can do well.

What's appealing about that approach is that you can buy a tiny home for around $60,000, or you can buy a kit from Home Depot for as little as $20,000 and build it yourself. Then, by renting it out on a nightly basis, I bet something like that could pay for itself inside two years. It could be a very cost-effective way to get into real estate investing, especially if you already own the land, or can find it in a desirable area for cheap.

Bringing Value to a Deal

If you have skills you can bring to a real estate deal, you just need to find investors with money, so you can partner. Two of the best avenues to connect with money people, outside of networking in investors' circles, are:

- **Real estate agents.** Agents always have clients who are interested in properties.
- **Property managers.** Property managers are also aware of which investors are ready to sell off a property or two, or can act as a go-between to explore potential opportunities.

One of my clients is always bird-dogging deals to create a path for long-term wealth and be able to jump out of the nine-to-five. She was asking me one day who I knew in the area that had some deals going. I told her about one of my other clients, who has too much land right now and is looking to possibly bring in an investor or a partner who can add value. I put the two of them in touch through a friendly introductory text message and they are talking about building a small apartment complex.

Remember, asking someone you know can always open a door, whether it is your lawyer, accountant, real estate agent, property manager, or BJJ colleague.

Once you connect with potential partners, you then need to demonstrate that you have knowledge or skills that will be useful to them.

Bird-Dogging Properties

Bird-dogging means driving around in search of properties that look like they could be candidates for purchase. For example, you could spot a zombie property that has obviously been sitting vacant for some time, or maybe just looks like it's vacant. You could drop a flyer off that asks, "Are you interested in talking about selling your house?" Or, you could take note of the address, research who the owner is, and mail them a postcard asking the same thing. Some potential buyers even craft handwritten notes.

My wife and I received four postcards last week about a property we have in Knoxville. Now, we're not interested in selling that particular house, but the fact that we're being contacted about it means there are people out bird-dogging deals.

In general, it's a numbers game, so the more postcards or letters you send out to property owners, the better your odds of someone being interested in talking with you about selling.

In addition to driving around and taking notes, you can also do the following research from your desk, by looking at:

- For Sale by Owner listings
- MLS listings
- Zillow
- Tax sales
- Foreclosures

Once you've identified a property that would be possible to buy and make money on, it's time to find your money people. That's when you start working to find someone who wants in on the deal you've found. Typically, 5% is a decent equity percentage to go for, but it's a negotiation, so you could go as high as 10%, though any higher than that and you may be getting a little greedy and lose out on an opportunity.

Wholesaling Properties

Wholesalers are another potential way to get into investing if you have some money to invest. Wholesalers buy contracts and flip them. That is, they make an offer on a property, put the deposit down, and then sell the contract to another buyer.

This can work if you find an undervalued property and get it under contract, and then turn around and try to resell it to investors at a price higher than what you are going to pay for it.

A variation of this worked for my client from New York, who was in the process of buying a property down here in Tennessee for $353,000. But she decided it wasn't the right time to move and wanted out of the contract. I called my real estate agent to see who he might know who would want to buy it. I told him, "I have a client house in Spring Hill. She's under contract for $353,000 and is closing in two weeks and wants out. Do you want to buy it?"

He said, "Yeah, I'll buy it for $400,000."

"I need higher than that," I told him.

"Let me go to my hedge fund," he said, and the hedge fund ended up buying it for $433,000.

My client ended up walking away with $93,000 having never made a mortgage payment. She unintentionally wholesaled the deal.

There's a whole industry out there dedicated to real estate wholesaling. You can learn more at BiggerPockets, which has a section on the platform specifically for wholesaling.

Underwriting the Project

To decide whether a real estate deal makes sense for you, you need to have someone underwrite it, or work through all of the financials and the factors that impact its value. Not everyone knows how to run the numbers, so if you can learn underwriting, that can be the value that you bring to a deal.

One part of underwriting is looking at the numbers, such as the asking price, the property taxes, any HOA fees, and average rents in the area. You also need to factor in any repairs or maintenance that needs to be addressed before you can rent the property out. More technical terms for some of this information are the internal rate of return (IRR), the return on investment (ROI), cap rate, and CapEx, which we just talked about in a recent chapter. You'll want to run through those calculations to see how the property stacks up.

Then you need to assess the property's location. What kind of neighborhood is it in, is it on a busy street or a cul-de-sac, does it have a big yard, what are some comps in the area, what school district is it in and how are the schools rated, and what is the crime rate for the area? You can ask to see crime reports for the area, as well as property history, and insurance history.

As the underwriter, you're breaking the property down to find out if there are issues you can't see from the surface, like whether there was ever a fire in the house, or it's in a flood plain. Those affect the property's value, which can affect what you rent it for.

I was recently looking at properties listed on BiggerPockets and came across a 3-bedroom, 2-bathroom townhouse in Memphis for $145,000, which is being rented for $900/month. The projected rent going forward is $1,100, however.

Even before you start looking closely at the property, I can tell you that this deal wouldn't work for me, simply because of the 1% rule. If the purchase price of the property is $145,000, I need to generate at least $1,450/month in rent, and tenants aren't anywhere close to that right now, or even forecasted for the future. So that would be a "no" from me.

But if you could buy it for $125,000 and get the rent up to $1,250, it might be worth looking at as an appreciation play. Meaning, you buy it and increase rents each year while the property itself is also appreciating. That's a longer-term investment opportunity that can work if you're willing to wait to flip it.

The process of running these numbers is underwriting, and if you're good at it, that can be the value you bring to a project that could net you some equity in the deal.

So, let's look at another potential listing as an example. This one, also on BiggerPockets, is in Chattanooga and is a 1,500-square-foot, 3-bedroom, 1-bath property that the seller is asking $135,000 for, with projected rent of $1,800. On the surface that looks like a good deal. After all, $1,800 is well over the 1% guideline.

But when you step back and look at the area that this particular property is in, you notice that it's not in the best neighborhood. The schools also aren't great. But what *is* great is the redevelopment that's going on there. Money is being spent to bring in big box retailers and restaurants, which is going to make this a more desirable area to live in.

Pooling Your Money

If you have a little bit of money, you could also explore syndication, maybe with some friends or colleagues. Similar to an investment club, where everyone puts in the same amount, maybe on a regular basis, you put the money in its own LLC. Then the LLC becomes a limited partner in a bigger syndication deal.

Managing the Project

The final way that someone who doesn't have money to invest can contribute and earn equity is by managing the property once it's purchased. If you're the property manager, you're the person who picks up the phone when tenants call about a leaky toilet or a refrigerator that won't keep food cold, as well as the person who goes to investigate and repair the toilet and refrigerator, or who makes arrangements for someone else to come out and repair them. You're the laborer, while your partner is the money.

In exchange, you'll receive, on average, about 5% of the profit each month, or whatever percentage you're able to negotiate.

If you're in the position where you'd like to start real estate investing but you don't expect to have more than a few thousand dollars to invest in the near future, start networking. Get to know real estate agents, go to BiggerPockets Meetups, and introduce yourself to property managers and tell everyone that you're getting into real estate investing and you'd welcome the chance to get involved in any deals they're exploring. You can be the bird-dog, or the underwriter, or the handyman, depending on your particular skills.

While you wait to find that first project, explore different ways to get some extra money coming in that you can set aside for investing down the line.

Key Takeaways

- Ask people about deals.
- Don't sit on the couch, get out there and meet people through Meetups, at the gym, or at the coffee shop. Real estate investors are some of the best people you can meet; they want you to succeed.
- What are your skillsets? If you cannot identify one off the top of your head, learn to underwrite. Knowing the numbers is critical to any deal.
- Real estate investing can involve outside-the-box investing with tiny homes, mobile home parks, self-storage units, and even travel trailers. Think outside the box.

CHAPTER 11

MANAGING THE PROPERTY

As soon as you purchase and own a rental property, one of your very first decisions should be whether to hire a property manager or to manage it yourself. There are pros and cons to each that you'll want to evaluate, to make sure that the income you earn from your property requires the least amount of time and effort on your part. After all, you probably aren't getting into real estate because you want a second or third job, right?

If your hope is that your real estate is going to create a steady stream of income, without many hours of extra work, you'll want to look into hiring an individual or a property management firm to help manage your real estate.

Hiring a Property Manager

Finding and retaining the right property manager is, hands down, the most important decision you'll make when working to build your residential real estate portfolio. A property manager is going to free your time to devote to finding other properties, closing deals, or working your day job. And if you don't live close to your rental property, hiring a manager is essential.

I'm a lawyer based in Tennessee. It doesn't make financial sense for me to hop on a plane, fly to Missoula, Montana, to clean the hot tub after a guest leaves our property there, and then turn around and fly all the way back home to Tennessee. While I might save a $100 cleaning fee by doing that, the cost of the roundtrip flight and my time is much more than $100.

Even if the property were two hours away, spending four hours roundtrip driving, plus an hour or more on-site, to take care of cleaning or showing the property still doesn't make sense, when you take into consideration the time value of money. Your time has value and, for most people looking to get into real estate investing, doing everything yourself is not making the best use of that time.

Fortunately, property managers can take care of more than just outsourcing the cleaning of your property. They also:

- Take care of paying property taxes
- Hire snow removal services
- Pay for lawncare and cleanup
- Hire pool maintenance, if needed
- Take care of hot tub servicing
- Pay for any pest or insect control
- Hire trash removal services
- Arrange for any interior maintenance and repairs (such as dishwasher breaking or roof leaking)
- Distribute the key along with any welcome instructions and gifts
- Regularly survey the property for any damage caused by guests or seasonal weather

Knowing that you have a professional keeping an eye on your building does reduce the stress associated with owning an out-of-state property. Your property manager knows when something needs repairing, such as when the gravel needs replacing on the unpaved driveway after being washed out during the winter, or when overhanging trees need to be cut back. Looking at property photos doesn't give you that context, to recognize what issues have emerged and need addressing.

Good property managers really do manage the property 24/7 so that you don't have to worry about what's happening when you're not there.

So, what does a good property manager look like? How can you recognize them? There are several questions I ask when I'm hiring a property manager for short-term rentals, including:

- How many doors do you have under management?
- What is your response time after receiving a call from a tenant?
- What fees do you charge?
- What services do you provide for that fee?
- What platforms are you on?
- How long have you been in business?
- Do you have a good following/a base of people who come to you for rentals?
- What type of property is the easiest for you to rent?
- Are there any types of properties you won't take on?
- What's a typical rent rate for a property like mine?
- Do you handle welcome gifts? What typically goes into them?
- How fast can you turn a property?
- Do you provide bedding and towels, or do we need to?
- How often are you checking on the property?

For long-term rentals, I also want to know:

- How many units do you have under management?
- What is your typical demographic?
- Do you specialize mainly in A, B, or C properties?
- How do you handle maintenance requests?

- What does your standard lease look like?
- Who do you use for evictions?
- What kind of deposits are you taking? Do you require a security deposit?
- Do you require everyone in a house to be on a lease?

The way the property manager gets paid for the minor issues that arise is that you, as the property owner, put money on deposit with the company to pay for needed repairs. In our experience, we pay, on average, $1,000 per door as a deposit. And the property manager can use that money to pay for minor incidents, like changing the locks after a long-term tenant leaves, or having the exterior windows cleaned in the spring. Anything under $250 they can pay for without asking you, but over $250, you want them to ask your permission first. Because at over $250, that's an issue you want to be aware of; they can't spend more than $250 without asking first. Then they replenish what they've spent during the month from the rents received next month.

If you have a good property manager, you should be getting money deposited in your bank account each month, with reasonable maintenance issues taken care of, like leaky faucets or a running toilet that won't stop.

Sending You Business

On top of maintaining your rental property, skilled property managers have a book of clients they have worked with in the past, and can direct them to your property as an option if they're looking for a place in your general area. Those connections and relationships can be really helpful, to be able to connect potential renters with you, especially if you've recently acquired a property and don't have a history of renters to rely on. Those relationships can mean the difference between a profitable property and one that sits vacant.

Preventing Bigger Problems

Skilled property managers also help reduce losses due to nonpaying renters. Since the managers are paid based on the rents they collect from tenants, it is in their best interest to ensure everyone pays, and pays on time. Part of their responsibility is to collect what is owed on your behalf, and then pass along what you are owed, minus their fee.

Although property managers are critical for short-term rentals, like Airbnb or Vrbo units, it's possible you could get by managing your own long-term rental. Because in those situations, you may turn over the unit once a year and then want to go in and spruce it up before you re-rent. As an annual activity, you may decide to manage that. I've personally handled cutting the grass here and there on our local properties because it didn't make sense to pay a huge fee to a property manager.

Once you own more than about five properties, at that point you may need a maintenance crew on-hand. You can hire a maintenance person who can stay busy addressing issues that routinely arise, as well as cutting the grass or shoveling sidewalks, but even at five properties, you probably wouldn't need them full-time. So maybe you hire a part-time handyman plus a lawn crew until you have enough properties to justify hiring your maintenance pro full-time.

As you scale, by adding more properties to your portfolio, you'll want to consider transitioning to a property management firm, versus hiring multiple maintenance people to cover multiple properties. You don't want to have to oversee multiple employees and at that point, maybe at ten or twelve properties in a single area, you should begin interviewing property management firms.

Dealing with Tenants who Don't Pay

A property manager shows his or her true worth when tenants get behind on their rent payments; typically, this only applies to long-term tenants, since short-term tenants pay in advance. Skilled property management firms keep a close eye on tenants who seem to be getting behind in their rent payments, or who are paying later and later each month. Most notify the tenant immediately that late payments are not acceptable and take steps to start evicting once it becomes clear the tenant can't pay. These issues should not become your issues, however, since that is why you pay, on average, 10% of your gross receipts to a manager. What you really want to avoid is having to officially evict a tenant, because it can take months, during which time you aren't collecting any rent. The key is to get slow-paying tenants out quickly, even if you have to pay to entice them to go.

You don't want to have to evict anyone, partly because you feel bad for telling them they have to move and partly because that means you've lost money for several months already. And evictions can be time-consuming and challenging; they aren't slam-dunks.

Eviction processes vary by city and state, so there is no one-size-fits-all guidance I can provide here. For example, in the state of Tennessee, we have the Tennessee Uniform Landlord Tenant Act. But it only applies to counties with a certain population size—above 300,000 residents—which includes major cities in the state, like Chattanooga, Knoxville, Nashville, Memphis, and now Franklin, and a few other counties.

In the cities and counties where the Tennessee Uniform Landlord Tenant Act does apply, you have to give tenants notice to quit. Meaning, you issue a notice that the tenant either needs to pay their rent in fourteen days or an eviction filing will be made. Then you have to wait the fourteen days to see if they do pay. If not, you file the detainer warrant (See Appendix for a sample) and wait for the next court date, usually within a few weeks, when you can get into court to ask for possession of your property back. In Tennessee, tenants then have ten days to vacate, with or without the help of a sheriff, if you want.

Evictions are called detainer actions because what you're doing is taking your property back. But even when you do get your property back, it is often in rough shape because the tenant wasn't happy that you forced them to leave. You'll probably have to invest some cash to get it cleaned up and repaired before you re-rent it.

Some property owners will attempt to sue the (former) tenant for past-owed rent, but if they don't have the money, they don't have it. You can get a judgment against them, and if you invest some time, you may be able to discover where they work and garnish their wages to get your money. However, I don't encourage you to do that. Rather than investing time and money to get a couple of months of rent back—which may be less than what your attorney charges you for their counsel—move on.

It's also important to keep in mind that, in general, laws are tenant-friendly, which means it may be difficult for you to force your non-paying tenants out in a timely manner. Eviction moratoriums during the pandemic, for example, made it more difficult for landlords to get non-paying tenants to move. Keep this in mind before you invest lots of money trying to fight it out in court. It could get expensive to have tenants removed.

My wife and I recently discovered a company called Rhino (SayRhino.com). It is a rent insurance company for property owners. The tenants pay the monthly premium and when they don't pay their rent, the landlord can make a claim and be made whole within days. We are just starting to use this company, so check back on my website later to see how it's going. If things go well, this could be transformative for property owners and landlords alike. Moreover, it allows the tenants an option of paying a small monthly fee in lieu of a security deposit.

"Keys for Cash"

One strategy some real estate owners use to entice tenants who are behind in their payments to leave is called "keys for cash." Essentially, you offer them an amount of money— maybe $200, maybe $500, depending on what the rent rate is—if they will move out today and hand over their keys to you. Tell them that you'll be there watching them move and that you'll hand them $500 in cash when they're done.

Don't give them the money until they're out and you have the key in-hand—which is going to be changed immediately, of course—but this tactic does often work. And it's a way to avoid the whole legal process, which is likely to cost you more than the cash you're offering your tenant.

I have a client who used this strategy to get a tenant out, in fact. My client had just sold his building, which had a former lawyer living in it who hadn't paid rent in forever. He owed my client a ridiculous sum of money—something like $12,000.

So, we filed the eviction and my client authorized me to offer him $10,000 to get out by a certain date. And he jumped on that offer and moved out. The funny thing is, a few weeks later, he asked for his security deposit back. Of course, I explained that wasn't the deal. "We paid you $10,000 to vacate the premises, but you don't get your security deposit back."

"Keys for cash" tends to work because if people aren't paying rent, they need the money. They would much rather take your money, without having to pay you any back rent, and move on.

Should You Consider Being Your Own Property Manager?

My wife and I use professional property management firms for all of our out-of-state properties because we know we can't be more responsive from hundreds of miles away than a local business. However, we're now rethinking that strategy after receiving a bill for the management of our Montana property. As we were reviewing the charges for the past month, we spotted a bill for three 12-packs of beer as a "welcome package." Now, our welcome package is a free bottle of wine for each renter, but not thirty-six beers.

We've also spotted a "guest fee" on the bill. That's not something we charge our renters, so it's unclear why we, the property owner, are being charged this by the property manager. That's a little suspicious.

So, while it makes sense to rely on an out-of-state property manager to handle cleaning your property and preparing it for your next guests, as well as maintenance and addressing any renter concerns, make sure you're going through your statement with a fine-tooth comb. Many of the charges you pass along to renters, such as cleaning fees, for example, should be more than covered by them. For example, we charge guests $150 for cleaning after they leave, but we pay $90 for the cleaning service. It should never actually cost you money for some of those services. You should come out positive.

Automating Property Management

We have recently started using an online platform created specifically to help property owners manage their own properties. It is called Buildium.

With Buildium, tenants download the app and can pay their rent online. You can pay cleaners or lawn workers or maintenance people through Buildium. And Buildium does the accounting for you and tracks income and expenses. So far, it's phenomenal, and it's saving us ten percent a month on property management fees, which more than pays for the software.

My client Winston and his wife Christi bought an apartment complex on the Alabama/Tennessee border, tore it down to the studs, and rebuilt all 140 units. They're now rented and he's using Buildium to manage them, with great success. He's the person who recommended it to me because it made his life so much easier.

So, if you decide to start by managing your own properties, seriously consider relying on an online platform for support. It will reduce the amount of time you spend following up on rent owed and paying bills to your suppliers or servicepeople.

That's my goal for you: to find residential properties that you can start renting quickly, so that you begin to generate income for yourself, without having to spend a lot of money to do so. That's what we all want, isn't it? We want a means of supplementing our current income that doesn't become another full-time job, because we don't have time for that.

My wife and I are working hard to acquire properties that we can rent out so that in the near future, we're earning enough to replace our day jobs. I'm not sure that we'll immediately quit our day jobs, honestly, but to have the flexibility to do that is the goal.

I want you to have those kinds of options, too!

Key Takeaways

- You can self-manage your properties when you own only one or two if you're willing to take calls from tenants. You'll save money, but it will be more time-consuming.

- Property managers save time, money, and effort in exchange for a percentage of the income you receive from each unit.

- Having someone who can take care of all issues, big or small, is important for keeping your properties delivering income regularly.

- Evictions of non-paying tenants are time-consuming and costly because you aren't collecting payments while you work to relocate them. Avoid them if you can.

CHAPTER 12

---···---

MAXIMIZING BUSINESS DEDUCTIONS

O ne of the biggest advantages of setting up a company to hold
your property is the ability to deduct any expenses associated
with running your business—and they can add up! Of course, you can
track and deduct expenses associated with a rental property whether
you own it within an LLC or S corp, but if your properties are the
asset of a company, you can deduct even more expenses associated
with their management and upkeep.

Business Expenses

As a real estate business owner, you can deduct most of the products
and services you use to manage your business. The more deductions,
the lower your taxable income, which is always good. According to
the IRS, here is what qualifies as business expenses:

(a) **In general** There shall be allowed as a deduction all the
ordinary and necessary expenses paid or incurred during
the taxable year in carrying on any trade or business,
including—

(1)
a reasonable allowance for salaries or other compensation

for personal services actually rendered;

(2)

traveling expenses (including amounts expended for meals and lodging other than amounts which are lavish or extravagant under the circumstances) while away from home in the pursuit of a trade or business; and

(3)

rentals or other payments required to be made as a condition to the continued use or possession, for purposes of the trade or business, of property to which the taxpayer has not taken or is not taking title or in which he has no equity.

For purposes of the preceding sentence, the place of residence of a Member of Congress (including any Delegate and Resident Commissioner) within the State, congressional district, or possession which he represents in Congress shall be considered his home, but amounts expended by such Members within each taxable year for living expenses shall not be deductible for income tax purposes. For purposes of paragraph (2), the taxpayer shall not be treated as being temporarily away from home during any period of employment if such period exceeds 1 year. The preceding sentence shall not apply to any Federal employee during any period for which such employee is certified by the Attorney General (or the designee thereof) as traveling on behalf of the United States in temporary duty status to investigate or prosecute, or provide support services for the investigation or prosecution of, a Federal crime.

In short, businesses can deduct expenses that are necessary to operate a trade or business. Here is a short list of the types of expenses you should be tracking and claiming as business deductions:

- Auto expenses—actual or the IRS's standard calculation per mile, which was set at $.56 as of 2021
- Expenses of going into business—which is limited to $5,000 in the first year, but after the business is operational, then advertising, utilities, rent, and repairs are deductible
- Legal and professional expenses
- Travel expenses
- Business travel
- Equipment
- Charitable contributions
- Taxes—sales tax, excise & franchise taxes, fuel taxes, employment taxes, state income taxes can be itemized on your federal return, and real estate taxes, as well as assessments
- Education expenses for things such as continuing education or maintaining your license, if applicable
- Advertising and promotion—websites, business cards, yellow page ads, etc.
- Pass-through deductions—sole proprietorships, partnerships, S corps, LLCs, and LLPs can deduct up to 20% of their net income, if they qualify

Additionally, there are other, often overlooked deductions that you don't want to miss out on, including:

- Bank service charges
- Business association dues
- Business gifts

- Business-related magazines and books
- Casual labor and tips
- Casualty and theft losses
- Cell phone and landline telephone service
- Coffee and beverage service
- Commissions
- Consultant fees
- Credit bureau fees
- Office supplies
- Parking and meters
- Petty cash funds
- Postage
- Seminars and trade shows
- Taxi, bus, and Uber-type fares

The key to maximizing your deductions—by which I mean taking every legitimate business deduction the IRS expects you to take as a business owner—is to constantly be asking yourself whether what you're using or doing is related to running your business. Especially in the first few years, the answer is very likely to be "yes."

For example, I make calls on my cell phone when I'm out of the office, which makes my cell phone and the cell phone service deductible. When I put in AirPods to hear while I'm in a public place, I'm using them for business so, therefore, they are a business expense I should deduct. When I pull out my laptop to work in a coffee shop, I'm using it for business so it is a business expense I should deduct. Anything I use in relation to my work can be deducted. It's a new way of thinking, but it can save you lots of money.

Additionally, you can deduct interest paid on real estate investments. So, if you take out a commercial loan on a property, for example, you can take an interest deduction on that loan. There is currently a $10,000 limit on the deduction you can take on personal residential real estate, but there is no limit on commercially purchased properties.

Your goal in those first few years of business is to pay no taxes at all. You want to offset any revenue you earn with deductions, to reduce your tax obligation. Through the combination of depreciation on your properties and the expenses associated with getting your firm up and running, you should end up paying close to $0 in taxes. That should be your goal.

So, pay attention to how you're spending your time and what tools or resources you're relying on to do that. When you drive across town to check out a property, make sure you're making note of your mileage so you can deduct it or reimburse yourself personally for the travel. If you jot down notes in a notebook, that should be something your company paid for, not you personally. If you hand your business card to a potential seller, make sure your company has paid for the design and printing of those cards. If you take a potential investor out to lunch, pay for it with your business credit card so that you can expense at least part of that meal. And if you buy a window air conditioning unit for your office, a new chair for your desk, a painting for your office wall, those are all business expenses as long as they have been purchased to help you make money.

This does take a mindset shift, I'll admit. But as long as you pay attention to everything you are using to make money, you will find new deductions you might not have originally thought of. Your subscriptions to real estate-related magazines? Deduct them. Travel to a real estate investment conference? Deduct it. Books about real estate investing, including this one? Deduct it.

All businesses are required to pay taxes only on what they owe, which is why it's so important to track all the expenses of running your business. At the end of the year, it will brighten your outlook to know that those dollars spent to run your real estate business are dollars well spent. Your accountant can also confirm that you've claimed all the deductions you are entitled to and potentially suggest others to which you may qualify for.

Key Takeaways

- Setting up a company, versus owning real estate personally, allows you to deduct business expenses associated with running the business, which add up quickly.

- In fact, almost everything associated with running your business is deductible, from office supplies to cleaning supplies to wear-and-tear on your vehicle used to scope out potential properties.

- Deducting interest on property loan payments is a useful tool, but the rules vary based on whether the property is residential or commercial.

- Track everything you do so that you can deduct it.

- Your goal in the first few years of business is to pay no taxes at all.

CHAPTER 13

———ᘉ———

WHEN IS THE BEST TIME TO SELL?

As a lawyer, you know my response to the question, "When should I sell?" is going to be, "It depends." Because there is no pat answer; it depends on several things, the first of which is what your goals are. Why did you buy the property in the first place? Everyone's answer is different, which is why there will never be one answer to this particular question.

For example, if you bought a property through a tax sale with plans to flip it, the answer to the best time to sell is, "As soon as it's ready to put on the market." Or, if you bought a multifamily property and have been renting it out annually but you're ready to retire and don't want to manage it anymore, you could either hire a property manager and hang onto the real estate or you could sell it and deposit the proceeds in your retirement account. If you recently bought a property to use on Airbnb and have changed your mind, now may not be the best time to sell, honestly. Or maybe it is. You need to reflect on the reasons why you bought it and then run some numbers to see if you can make money if you sell right now.

A friend asked me that same question last week and my response to him, too, was, "It depends." And I told him the same thing I'm telling you—think back about why you bought this particular property, what you were hoping to gain, and what you would gain if you sold it right now. Does it still make sense to hold it? Or will selling it help you reach your real goal faster?

Only you can answer that. Determining when to sell a property depends on the goals you set for your real estate investing business.

Was Your Goal Long-Term Renting?

If you purchased a property in order to generate a regular monthly income—as is generally the case with long-term rental units—you need to compare what you would earn from the rental income with what you would earn by selling it. Essentially, you're looking at the inflection point of rental income to property value. Or, said another way, you're trying to determine the point at which the value of the property exceeds what you would earn from renting it.

Let's run through an example. Kim buys a three-bedroom, two-bath house for $200,000 in a nice suburb outside of a major city. The schools are highly rated, the crime rate is low, and property values continue to climb steadily, suggesting that this area will remain a strong bedroom community. Kim's tenant pays $2,250 per month in rent, which is above the 1% standard I told you about earlier. As a rental, it seems like a strong performer.

Here are the financials for the property:

Loan Amount: $160,000
Down Payment: $40,000
Insurance per Month: $100
Interest Rate: 3.5%
Term: 15 years
Monthly Payment: $1,143.81
Rent – Loan Payment = ($2,250-$1,143.81) = ($1,106.19
x 12) = $13,274.28 per year

What this tells us is that Kim generates a little more than $13,000/year in profits simply by holding the property and continuing to rent it out.

By Year 5, the property value has increased from $200,000 to $295,000. Kim has been depreciating the property under Section 179 of the tax code and has been able to deduct ordinary business expenses, such as we discussed in Chapter 11, under Section 162 of the tax code, and her monthly profit is consistent. The result is a nice year-end profit for Kim's initial investment.

However, using the 1% guideline to determine monthly rents, Kim should now be charging just under $3,000/month to keep pace, and the reality is that this area cannot sustain rental rates at that level for a three-bedroom, two-bath house. That figure is above average market rates.

So, if Kim sells her property for $295,000 in Year 5, she will recoup her initial $40,000 down payment, plus the property appreciation of $95,000 (meaning, the value that she has gained by owning it, as the value grew from $200,000 to $295,000), minus real estate agent fees of 6%, or $17,700. After selling, Kim would be left with $117,300 at closing, which is about ten years' worth of rental payments at the current rental rates. Said another way, it would take Kim ten years to earn that much money.

This is a good time to sell this property.

The reason that Kim might consider selling is that the recurring monthly rents will not keep up with the property value, so that Kim can continue to make a profit that is in line with the market. On the other hand, if the market could sustain an annual increase, to raise the rents to $3,000/month, then a better decision would be to hold on to the property, rather than sell it.

Was Your Goal Appreciation?

Now, if your goal in buying a property was either to fix and flip it, a BRRRR, or for forced appreciation, the calculation regarding when to sell that property changes. It's no longer dependent on monthly income, since the reason for buying it was to try to increase its value and then sell at a profit.

When an investor buys a property that is not cash flowing well and, at purchase, would not be categorized as a "good investment" by any metrics, but the investor then turns it around and creates profit, the amount of that newly created profit determines whether now is a good time to sell.

Let's use another example. Rick buys a quadplex in an area just outside a mid-sized city, which is seeing strong economic growth. The property itself needs some repairs, after which a rent increase can be justified.

Rick buys the property for $300,000, with each unit renting for $550/month, for a total rental income of $2,200/month.

However, Rick is planning to renovate and upgrade each unit at the end of each tenant's individual lease term. When the lease ends, he will turn it by replacing carpeting with luxury vinyl laminate flooring, replacing cabinet pulls and doorknobs with an updated style, and painting the walls. After making those enhancements, he will increase the rent by $100/month for the first year, and by 10% each year thereafter.

Here's what the monthly rents will look like going forward, per unit:

Year 1: $650
Year 2: $715
Year 3: $786.50
Year 4: $865.15
Year 5: $951.66

By Year 5, the property generates $3,806.64 per month, or $45,679.68/year, and the property is now worth $450,000. Thus, the cap rate for this property is:

$45,679.68÷$450,000 = 0.10

These are rough numbers, just to illustrate the example.

By Year 5, not only is the property cash flowing well, but the value of the property has also risen, thanks to minimal improvements made to each unit, which have added value beyond simple market appreciation. Rick increased the rent received by $401.66 per unit per month since purchasing the property in Year 1. So, if Rick had bought the property with a goal of increasing its value, that goal has been achieved. Between the cash flow improvement and increased property value, Rick has achieved significant appreciation for the quadplex.

Would now be a good time to sell the property?

Again, it depends on Rick's goals, really. He won't actually receive the value of the forced appreciation until he sells. Forced appreciation is generally a one-time benefit of the property. But by increasing the value of the property through rent increases, Rick will make his money on the sale, so he should consider selling the property now.

Other Factors that Might Make it Time to Sell

Dawn and I have a few duplexes in West Tennessee, and we have some friends who are interested in getting into real estate investing. Their long-term goal is passive income. Our properties are doing just fine, we are making our 1% each month and we don't need to sell. However, we could use that money on other projects.

So, Dawn and I agreed that we would sell the duplexes in an off-market deal to our friends for $15,000 more than we paid two years ago. Given the current seller's market, we could probably get more for them if we wanted, but pigs get fat and hogs get slaughtered, and always trying to get the most for something is sometimes greedy—we want to take our profits and move on.

We bought the properties from my client and friend, who sold them to me so I could meet a 1031 exchange deadline. He sold them to me for the appraised value, which saved me many thousands of dollars. He did not have to help me, but he did. It's now our turn to help someone else.

There is a lot of money to be made in real estate investing. Some you can make in the short-term, such as by fixing and flipping a property, or by Airbnb-ing a desirable vacation property. And some you can make long-term, such as by purchasing a property and holding it, to take advantage of price appreciation that many areas continue to witness, or by updating some or all of the units in order to be able to raise the monthly rent.

When to sell first comes down to your goals—and whether continuing to hold the property gets you closer to achieving them— and second, it depends on the market. The numbers should make sense before you agree to sell your investment.

My wife and I continue to add to our portfolio, because our goal is to get to a point where our rental income replaces our salaries. But that doesn't mean that we don't sell some properties from time to time, when we get an offer that makes sense. Then we turn around and buy other properties that get us closer to our goal.

Think about why you're getting into real estate investing, what you want to accomplish, and then take that first step. That's the best way to get closer to reaching that goal. Best of luck!

Key Takeaways

- Decide what your goals are for owning real estate, in order to make decisions to sell easier. If you're after income, for example, and your property isn't producing it, you may want to consider whether you should consider owning it.

- Reflect on what you were hoping to gain when you first bought the property, as well as what you have to gain by selling in order to decide whether to sell now.

- With rental properties, if the recurring monthly rents are not keeping up with the property value, it may be the right time to sell.

- Sometimes the best move is selling one property in order to generate cash to be able to invest in a different one is the best move.

RESOURCES

Residential real estate investing has really taken off in the last few years, which has led to a number of new online platforms and information sources springing up. Some are terrific and super helpful, and others are a complete waste of time, no matter where you are in your investing journey.

Here are some of the resources I turn to for continuing education about real estate investing. This is certainly not an exhaustive list, but I'm confident that the ones I rely on can help you, too. I've also included a list of some of the service providers I rely on, in case you want to explore working with them, too.

BOOKS
Buy, Rehab, Rent, Refinance, Repeat: The BRRRR Rental Property Investment Strategy Made Simple by David Greene
The Multifamily Millionaire, Volumes I and II, by Brian Murray and Brandon Turner
Profit First by Michael Michalowicz
Rich Dad Poor Dad by Robert Kiyosaki
The Road to Serfdom by F.A. Hayek

FACEBOOK GROUPS
Real Estate Investing for All

FINANCIAL MANAGEMENT
QuickBooks
Buildium

FORMS
Articles of Organization (link to website for sample)
Detainer Summons (link to website for sample)
Operating Agreement (link to website for sample)
Purchase and Sale Agreement (link to website for sample)

INSURANCE
SayRhino (tenants can pay and landlords can file a claim for nonpayment)
State Farm (for property insurance)

RENTAL PLATFORMS
AirDNA
Buildium
Rentometer

PODCASTS
BiggerPockets Real Estate Podcast
Best Real Estate Investing Advice Ever by Joe Fairless
Passive Wealth Strategy Show
Tax Smart Real Estate Investors Podcast

PROPERTY SOURCING
Crexi (for commercial property searches)
LoopNet (for commercial property searches)
Realtor
Redfin
Zillow

SERVICE PROVIDERS
Accountant: Allison Johnson
Banks: Pinnacle Financial Partners, Fourth Capital
Banker:
Todd Norman, Brian Shaw, Jr.

Carl Haynes
EVP – Chief Banking Officer
carl.haynes@lineagebank.com
615.804.5530
NMLS # 664762

BiggerPockets also has a list of providers, which can be found under the Network tab, where you can Build Your Team.

Please let me know about new resources you find that you think I should know about by emailing me at brian@briantboyd.com.

If you really want to leave your job and do this full-time, replacing your income and being your own boss, this book can help you get there.

ENDNOTES

1   https://www.bankrate.com/investing/
survey-favorite-long-term-investment-2021/

2   https://news.gallup.com/poll/349607/
americans-expect-home-prices-rise-divided-buying.aspx

3   https://news.gallup.com/poll/309233/
stock-investments-lose-luster-covid-sell-off.aspx

4   http://zillow.mediaroom.com/2022-01-27-U-S-housin
g-market-has-doubled-in-value-since-the-Great-Rece
ssion-after-gaining-6-9-trillion-in-2021

5   https://www.nytimes.com/2021/10/22/realestate/
single-family-rentals.html

6   https://news.airbnb.com/about-us/

7   https://www.phocuswire.com/2021-was-best-year-ever-fo
r-short-term-rentals